Where was God when...?

Real answers to hard questions.

MIKE CALHOUN & RIC GARLAND

Where Was God When...?

Real answers to hard questions

Published by Word of Life Fellowship, Inc.
P.O. Box 600
Schroon Lake, Ny 12870

www.wol.org

Please note: The authors have prepared a DVD video series to accompany this text. Information regarding the series is available is found in the back of this book.

Cover design by Natalie Cutting and Jon Eger
ISBN: 978-1-935475-10-1

www.wherewasgod.wol.org

Printed in the United States of America

Special thanks...

to those who allowed us to share their stories.

Contents

Contents

Chapter 1

Omniscience

Mike Calhoun

We've all been there, but some of us don't want to admit it. How could we be so bold as to question if God really cares? Many of us have walked through a time in our lives when we thought God had abandoned us. He saved us and had done nice things for us, but at that moment, He just wasn't there. There's a song by BarlowGirl that expresses that feeling perfectly. It says, "I waited for you today. But you didn't show."

We pray and feel like our prayers don't get above the ceiling. So we recoil inside as the hard questions envelop us in darkness. The questions are very real and the answers are not easy. But we are never going to find those answers if we aren't willing to deal with them head-on, looking to the Bible for answers. Are you ready?

God is infinite

As we try to work through these questions, one difficult truth is that God is infinite and we are not. He's got the big picture, but our vision is limited to a very small part of the equation. And so we doubt.

We ask things like, “God, why would You let this happen?” The answer is more than a Christian cliché that ends with happily ever after. This real, complex truth can be found in God’s Word, but it’s often not until we experience it that we realize this truth, when we see how it works in real life. Going through the process of personal trials and tragedy has brought me to the point of realizing that the only answer to some of the difficult questions of life is, simply, God.

I know that sounds like a cliché. It sounds too simple, but believe me, there is nothing simple about that answer. There are no easy explanations for some of the things that happen in our world, because our minds are so finite. So, in order to deal with reality, we have to go back to the attributes—or characteristics—of an infinite God. These attributes tell us what God’s character is like and help us understand the answers to some of our questions.

God is omniscient

Omniscience means *God knows everything*.

Now, let’s leave the explanation of that statement aside for a second and complicate it a little bit. If God knows everything, then why does He allow so many terrible things to happen?

- If God knows everything, why do I feel so alone?
- God, if You are really in charge, if You really know everything, then why do I question whether or not You even exist?
- God, if You know everything, then why did You let my friend commit suicide?
- If you know everything, then listen, God, I have a question for you. Why did You let that person abuse me?
- God, if You’re really in control and You really know everything, then why can’t I get rid of this secret sin?
- God, if You really know everything, why don’t You fix everything, and why don’t You just fix everybody? Because if I was God, that’s what I would do.

You're not the first one to ask these questions. I can tell you this: I have asked the same questions. But do you realize that even some people in the Bible asked the same questions? You are probably familiar with the story of Job. He was a man who went through some incredible hardships, including bankruptcy, the death of his children, and physical illness. Throughout it all, Job remained faithful to God. But in the midst of the difficulty, he also had three serious questions he sincerely asked God.

His first question was, "Why was I ever born?" He followed that one up with, "Why didn't you just let me die at birth?" And then his last question, "Why can't I die now?"

Maybe you've thought that way before. I'd like to share with you something I went through.

March 14, 2002, started out like most other days. I got up early, went to the airport, and caught a flight. On this day I was flying into Atlanta and then going up to Chattanooga, Tennessee. I had meetings all weekend, but I was going to begin my weekend by spending some time with my daughter. We planned to go to a Christian concert, attend her church together, and just hang out.

Little did I know that before I even caught the plane, my daughter Misty would already be dead and she'd be in eternity. She was in a 125-car pileup and was one of the only five people in the entire accident who were killed.

I recorded my feelings in a journal throughout the entire nightmare. Because I didn't know how to express my thoughts verbally, I wrote them down. One of the mornings right after she died, I wrote this: "I woke up at 3:55 this morning, and my first thought was, 'One week ago, I buried my baby. She was 24, but she was still my baby. It seems like it was just yesterday, but yet it seems like an eternity. Some days it feels like it is happening in the present. I sit here looking at her picture, and I still cannot believe that she is really gone, but I know she is. God, I just don't understand.'"

There are some questions that all of our Christian clichés just don't answer. A week from the day we put my daughter's body in the ground, I went for a long walk, still trying to wrap my mind around all of what I was experiencing.

It has now been several years since her home-going, and even though I love God, and I love the Bible and I read it every day, I'm still trying to wrap my mind around what happened and why.

There are some questions that don't have easy answers. I still believe the answer is God, but that doesn't mean it's easy. We all have to really wrestle with the truth about God right where we live, in the situations we face every day.

So, let me ask you a couple questions.

What is really the truth about God? If we're going to say that God is the answer to the hard questions, then what is the real truth about God? What does it mean when we say, "He is omniscient"?

I'm going to give you some ideas, because when we talk about God knowing everything, I don't want you to simply say, "Oh, that's just one of those Bible things," and then move on. I want to take the time to help you understand what it means.

Saying that God knows everything means that He possesses perfect knowledge. That means He knows everything, and He knows it correctly. He doesn't just know *that* it is; He knows totally *what* it is and *why* it is.

He has no need to learn

God has never learned and will never learn. If He can learn, He's not God. You and I are constantly learning, but God has never learned anything. God perfectly knows Himself. Even at my age, I am still discovering myself, and some things I discover I don't like. But God never discovers anything about Himself since He knows Himself perfectly. And He never discovers anything about us He already doesn't know.

God knows instantly and effortlessly all things. As humans, we know a great deal, but we do not know the future. God knows everything from the beginning to the end, so He knows the future. He knows all the variables that are going to happen. Not only that, He knows all the variables that *could have* happened. That's a lot to wrap our minds around.

I wonder about the variables on March 14, 2002, when my daughter was killed. What if her dog had not run away and made her leave late for work? I wonder if she had been on time, like she normally was—would she have been ahead of the accident and still be alive? I wonder what would be different if she had stopped to get a cup of coffee.

As you know, I was flying to be with her, so what if I had gone the day before—would she still be alive? If I had been there, I could have said to her, "Why you don't take the day off?" I could have said to her, "I'll go find the dumb dog."

See, we can chase those variables around all we want to, but here's the thing we have to understand: God is the only One Who knows all things and my mental gymnastics will only lead to more questions.

Isaiah 57:1-2 gave me great comfort after my daughter died. The message of those verses is powerful. It says that sometimes God takes young people to spare them from the pain, agony, and tragedy that is to come.

God is omniscient. He is never surprised; He is never amazed; He never wonders at anything.

One of my morning disciplines is to meditate on one of God's attributes. It's been a great journey of discovery and learning. I have found some very practical truths that are meaningful to me. One day I wrote, "God never says 'oops' or 'oh no.'"

I am constantly saying, "Oh, no!" or ,"Oops, I wish I hadn't done that." God never says that, because He knows everything.

God knows us completely. That's scary! God knows everything about us, from our beginning to our end.

I cannot tell you that my time of meditating on God has answered all of my questions, but I can tell you it has changed my perspective.

Jeremy Camp wrote a song where he reminds us that we can walk by faith, even when we can't see. But this faith is only possible when we put our trust in *Who God is*.

So what is omniscience? What does it tell us about Who God is? Let's start with what the Bible says about God and His omniscience. Let's examine some verses together to help us with this concept.

Isaiah 40:13-14 says this:

> "Who has directed the Spirit of the LORD,
> Or as His counselor has taught Him?
> With whom did He take counsel, and who instructed Him,
> And taught Him in the path of justice?
> Who taught Him knowledge,
> And showed Him the way of understanding?"

Who has directed the Spirit of the Lord? Who is His counselor? Who taught God? Where did God go to school? God doesn't have any class rings. Nobody taught God. If you look down to the very end of the passage it asks, "Who taught Him knowledge?" Nobody.

"Who showed Him understanding?" Nobody.

God knows everything already.

Isaiah 46:9-10 says:

> "Remember the former things of old,
> For I am God, and there is no other;
> I am God, and there is none like Me,
> Declaring the end from the beginning,
> And from ancient times things that are not yet done,
> Saying, 'My counsel shall stand,
> And I will do all My pleasure.'"

God says, "I know the end from the beginning. I know everything that is going to happen." It's one thing to make this claim, but it's another thing altogether for such a statement to be true. When God says He knows everything and is in control of everything, it's true. He does, and He is.

Here is a great passage that gives us some practical insight. Psalm 139:1-6 says:

> "O LORD, You have searched me and known me.
> You know my sitting down and my rising up;
> You understand my thought afar off.
> You comprehend my path and my lying down,
> And are acquainted with all my ways.
> For there is not a word on my tongue,
> But behold, O LORD, You know it altogether.
> You have hedged me behind and before,
> And laid Your hand upon me.
> Such knowledge is too wonderful for me;
> It is high, I cannot attain it."

"You have searched me and you have known me." He knows when we sit down; He knows when we get up, and what we're thinking. That ought to motivate us to godly living as well as give us great security. He says He knows everything about you. David wrote, "You're acquainted with all my ways."

Matthew 6:8 says, "Therefore, do not be like them for the Father knows the things you have need of before you ask Him."

God knows everything. He knows what you need. So let's put that truth to the test and look at a hard question. If God knew what I needed, then why did He let my daughter die?

I don't know, but I do know God. And I know that because He knows all things, He doesn't make mistakes.

Acts 15:8 says, "So God, who knows the heart, acknowledged them by giving them the Holy Spirit, just as He did to us." He knows our hearts.

Psalm 147:4 says, "He counts the number of stars; He calls them all by name." As humans, we are still discovering the universe, and just when we think we have it figured out, we realize there's more. God knows all the stars, and He's already taken care to give them all names.

In Jeremiah 38:17-20, Jeremiah is talking to Zedekiah. He says this, "Please, obey the voice of the LORD which I speak to you. So it shall be well with you, and your soul shall live." God knows all things, so why would we not listen to Him?

Colossians 1:16-17 says, "For by Him all things were created that are in heaven and that are on earth, visible and invisible, whether thrones or dominions or principalities or powers. All things were created through Him and for Him. And He is before all things, and in Him all things consist."

He created the world, and He holds it all together. That is what the passage means when it says, "By Him all things consist." In the back of our minds, we have a nagging fear that the world is going to end. We fear terrorist attacks, meteorites, a nuclear holocaust, but God created the world, and He holds it together. One of these days God will say, "OK, that's it. We're done." Then the God Who holds the universe in His hand is just simply going to turn it loose. But until then, we have nothing to fear because the world is in His hands.

One of the verses that I've come to know recently is Hebrews 4:13. It says, "Nothing in all creation is hidden from God's sight. Everything is uncovered and laid bare before the eyes of him to whom we must give account" (NIV). Nothing ever happens behind God's back.

So let me ask you this question: How does this apply to you? What difference does it make if God is really omniscient? If you are dealing with hard life questions, then you know there are no easy answers. Knowing that God is omniscient does not minimize your problems, but it will help you maximize your God.

I'm not saying to you, "Oh, it's OK; it's not a big deal," because it *is* a big deal. But the only place we can find comfort and answers is in the person of God. That's why we really want to understand these truths, and why we want them to be part of our lives. So how can you apply this truth to your personal life? I'm going to give you four words to help make this application.

1. Security. Consider what this means. Because God knows everything, because He knows us completely, that means that

God will never discover anything about you or me that will turn Him against us. Have you ever had a friend who, when he found out something about you, said, "OK, that's it, we're done"? Not God! There is nothing that will turn Him against us.

One of my favorite writers, A.W. Tozer, says this, "No talebearer can inform on us, no enemy can make his accusation stick, and no skeleton can come tumbling out of some hidden closet to turn Him against us." Basically, what he is saying is that there is nothing that God could ever discover about us that would cause Him to abandon us. The reason why is because He knew all about us in advance.

Remember how Jesus died for us and paid the price for our sin? The Bible says that He loved us while we were "yet sinners" (Romans 5:8). He knew everything I was going to do. He knew everything you were going to do. He knew all the terrible things. He knew that as a believer, we were going to fail sometimes. In light of all that, He still cared for us.

2. Comfort. When we are faced with some unexplainable circumstance in our life, we can trust God and find comfort. There are times when there's no human who can help you. A friend can put his or her arm around you, love you, pray for you, and do everything humanly possible. But there are times when the pain inside of you is so great that no one on the outside can do anything to help you on the inside.

You know what I mean. You've had those times when no person could help that ache inside you. Many times since the day my daughter went home to be with Jesus, my wife and I have journaled, and in many of those journals I've written sentences such as, "God, there is a hole in my soul. Every day there is this great big vacuum in my life." I have some great friends, but they can't fill that hole. Only God can!

3. Direction. In relationship to everyday living, I talk to Christians frequently who say, "I just don't know what to do. I really want my life to count for God, but this whole thing of knowing how to live for God is tough. I don't get it!"

Here's the good news—are you ready for this? God knows everything. If God knows everything, then He knows the dangers ahead of us as well as the joys. He knows the way and He can provide the wisdom we need. We need to trust Him to give us clear direction for our lives.

Here's what we need to do: we need to listen and obey. When He warns us, we need to listen. When He instructs us, we need to learn. When He comforts us, we need to accept it. We go to God for direction because He knows everything.

Do you know why some of us don't follow Him? We're just not sure He's got a handle on things. In our little finite minds, it doesn't make sense, so we wonder if He's got it all together. It doesn't make sense that a young person would die. It doesn't make sense that someone at a young age would have cancer. It doesn't make sense that we would experience pain. Because we are limited, it just doesn't make sense.

4. Conviction. Since God knows everything about us, that should convict us if we are living a hypocritical life. Some Christians are living a masquerade, thinking they have everybody fooled. Perhaps everyone around us is deceived, but not God, because He knows all things.

One day we will all stand before God and the real truth about us will be exposed. Here's something that we need to understand: because God knows everything, there's no sin you and I commit that He doesn't know. We think that just because there's nobody with skin on around us, we're getting away with it.

This is not to say that God is some evil spy watching us to try and catch us in sin. Remember, He died for our sin, motivated by His great love and mercy. The reason He pays attention to sin in your life is so that you can have uninterrupted fellowship with Him, which you can't with sin. His knowing about your sin makes it that much easier to make things right with God, since you can't hide it. God is omniscient; that truth brings comfort to those who honor Him and conviction to those who do not.

God's omniscience means we have security, comfort, direction, and conviction. So, how are you going to process this in your life? What does this mean when you think about how you live every day?

Here are three things you can do with what I just said. You have to determine how you will apply and handle this truth.

You can compartmentalize. You can simply suppress the truth, saying that you don't believe it. You can try to block out the truth and say that you don't believe God is really like that. You can live in denial. When we do that, what we're really doing is creating our own version of God.

Instead of accepting Who the Bible says God is, we create our own God. We try to put God in a box.

If you and I try to bring God down to our level to fit in our little, finite minds—if we try to put Him in a box—it's not going to work. You can compartmentalize all day and suppress the truth. You can say, "Hey look, I don't feel comforted; I'm still confused. I'm just going to keep living like I want to." You can try to change your version of God to fit your reality, but I have news for you: God will never fit inside your box. Ignoring His truth won't make it go away.

You can spiritualize. You can acknowledge the truth. Now, this one sounds good, but in reality, this is just the adoption of Christian lingo. If you do this when terrible things happen in your life, you just say things like, "God is good." Well, He is. Or you say, "All things work together for good." It's easy to say these things, but in reality, you still don't have a clue what's happening. Don't get me wrong, God is good and He does have a bigger plan, but just using clichés will never be enough.

Vance Havner was one of the great preachers of the past. After his wife died, another preacher said, "I want you to know, Dr. Havner, that all things work together for good, and God is good." Dr. Havner replied, "Yes, God is good. That is true, and it will work out, but right now I am dying on the inside." I think Dr. Havner was facing life from a real perspective. God is good, but life still hurts.

When we simply spiritualize truth, we are acknowledging it with our head but not with our heart. To spiritualize truth is easier because we do not take the time to search it out and wrestle with it. If we want to really know God and really understand how to handle these tough situations, though, we need to not just give a mental assent. We need to spend time in the Bible, wrestling through these truths.

It's like believing a theory or a definition—you memorize it and move on without making any personal application. It's a generic thing, where one size fits all. But that is not the way God works in lives. He is interested in us personalizing our faith. He wants to show up in *your* life, for you to know Him better.

God has given my wife and me a ministry with hurting parents who have lost children in death. One of the very first things we say to them is, "We don't know how you feel." You may think, "Sure, you do know how they feel, because your daughter died," but everybody has to process and grieve differently.

It is a personal journey with different feelings, processes, and circumstances, and God deals with us individually. The only thing that is constant is God.

You can internalize it. To internalize the truth is to believe the truth and to decide to trust God. It is taking what God has said about Himself and His Word and trusting that it is true, even in the midst of a horrible situation.

I have had people say to me that they could not trust God because they cannot see Him. But that same person may readily trust other people or things.

Let me illustrate. Almost every week of my life, I go to the airport, board an airplane, and fly somewhere to minister. I usually don't get on the plane and say to the flight attendant, "I'd like to see the pilot." I have never knocked on the door and asked to see his credentials. I don't check to see if he's drunk or sober.

I simply get on the plane and sit down. I actually strap myself in. I trust the pilot, whom I have never seen and do not know. He has never done anything to prove that he cares about me. So why is it so hard for us to trust God, Who knows everything and has proven His love to us by dying for us?

If you really want to get a handle on this truth and apply it to your life, then you need to internalize it. Begin by telling God how you feel and ask for His help. Ask Him to give you the strength to trust Him and keep the big picture.

There's another part to the story I told you earlier about my daughter's death:

I still don't understand all of it. I've prayed, I've read the Word. I have spent a lot of time considering this, but I still don't understand. I don't know that I will understand until I get to Heaven. But another one of the journal entries I made right after she died expresses my internalizing the truth.

> *"I went for a walk this morning to get some exercise. It was the first time since Misty had died. I meditated on Psalm 34, which says, "I will bless the Lord at all times, and His praise shall continually be in my mouth." Then I wrote these words, "Lord, all the time, yes, all the time, even during this time, I bless you and praise you for taking Misty home. My finite mind does not understand it, but as I have contemplated for many years Your attributes, I can say I believe that You are still all those things. I know that You are sovereign, You are holy, You are omniscient, You are omnipotent. I know that You are love. I know that You could have prevented this accident or incident. And I know that You, by Your design, allowed Misty to be taken home. My whole world has fallen apart. But everything I know about God is still true."*

Can you say the same?

Chapter 2

Immutability

Ric Garland

Think about some of the questions you may have in your head or your heart. You may be afraid to say them out loud, or they may be feelings you try not to think about because they are so painful. When have you wondered "Why?" or "Where was God?" when something tough happened?

In this chapter, we'll be looking at God being immutable, or His never changing nature. *Immutability* seems like a big concept meant to be thrown around in philosophy discussions—something that may be true about the God of the universe but doesn't have much to do with the problems you face every day.

I'm going to try to show you, though, what God's immutability means to you or your friends as you face tough situations. Let's look at some questions you or someone you know may be asking:

- Where was God when my parents were getting divorced?
- Why didn't I make the team?
- Why am I not as smart as they are?

- Why did my good friend commit suicide?
- Where was God when my pastor left because of sin?
- Why am I not developing as fast as other girls?
- Where was God when my grandma died?
- Where was God when I was molested by a relative?
- Why is God letting me flunk a class I need to pass?
- Why did I get dumped by the guy who said last night that he loved me?
- Where was God when I got slapped so hard by my drunk dad that I fell to the floor?
- Where was God when I kept coming home to an empty house?
- When I had sex?
- When I got bitter?
- When I get angry quickly?
- Where was God when I kept watching my mom get beat up by my step-dad?
- Why did my best friend, who calls herself a Christian, stab me in the back?
- Where was God when the dog we've had since I was born died?
- Where was God when I got raped?
- Tried to kill myself?
- Got drunk?
- Felt alone in a crowd?
- When I cut myself?
- Where is God when I have a secret life I regret?
- I stand up for truth and it only hurts me?

If God is really God, couldn't He stop these things? If He loves me, wouldn't He want to keep them from happening? If He's powerful, can't He change them?

Why does God allow children to get molested? Where is He when people get divorced? What about Christians who do terrible things?

We've heard about God being all-powerful, all-knowing, and unchanging in Sunday school since we were little. So why doesn't He stop it? Where is God when all this terrible stuff happens?

The answer is that God is there, and He does care about people who have these questions, but hearing that doesn't make it easier. We have a need to understand better Who God actually is, and why—since He loves us—this still happens.

Let me share about something that happened in my life. Like you, it made me question, "Where was God?"

> *When I was in college, I loved spending time with people, and especially dating girls. I never got serious with any of them—what guy does when he's young? One day my mother wanted me to meet this girl. Right, I thought, I'm going to meet a girl that my mom wants to introduce me to. It was New Year's Eve and I was home. We went to the church and she introduced me. Well, I hate to admit it but, uh...she was pretty. She was smart, witty, challenging, engaging, and we just hit it right off. I fell in love with Karen, and my life changed, with this amazing girl becoming a big part of it.*
>
> *Our relationship went up and down. We got close and then she backed away. We got close and she backed away. I was still in college, and she was teaching at a Christian school. When she decided she was going to go to Japan and teach some missionary kids for a couple of years, I thought it was great, but once she was gone, my heart broke. I had to tell her the truth. So, I wrote her a letter and told her I loved her. Right at that time she came up with some physical problems that complicated some things emotionally and spiritually, and she had to come home.*

At the same time, I was a missionary and was attending a missions conference an hour and half from home. After it was over, my dad and a friend met me in the back. My dad took me down to an office and told me that Karen had put a noose around her neck, kicked a chair out from underneath herself, and hung herself that morning.

Have you ever had that knot in your stomach that you couldn't get rid of? Did you ever feel the pain so hard that you couldn't explain it to anybody? I felt that. I felt that rejection.

I remember for weeks afterward driving down the road and literally seeing her hanging from a noose, calling out my name.

Where was God? I was supposed to marry her. I loved her. Why did God let that happen?

As I was trying to grapple with my feelings and where God fit in, I ran into some friends who told me that when Karen was found hanging there, finger marks were found on her neck. At the last minute, while she was choking, she changed her mind—but it was too late.

Do you ever say, "God, how can you let one of your children do that? How can you do that?" Why would God let that happen?

It happened almost twenty-seven years ago. I'm still asking those questions. You may ask, "How do you handle that?" Well, I'm going to show you in this chapter. For me, the Sunday school answers—that God is all-powerful, all-knowing, immutable—didn't change the hurt or the questions I had. I had to learn for myself Who God really was, and why—since He loved me—this could still happen.

My hope is that I can use what I learned to give you a better understanding of where God is when you have those hard questions.

I believe God has an answer—maybe not the answer you want, but God has an answer. This answer is found in the truth about God, or specifically *Who* He is. We have to look at God's *character*. Just like we would think of a person's reputation by who they are and what they do, we can know Who God is by looking at His *attributes*, or characteristics of Who He is.

This chapter's attribute, immutability, means God never changes.

When we think about the fact that God never changes, think about you. We change our mind, change our clothes, change our habits, change our thoughts, change our ways, change our will, change our sleeping habits, change our relationships, change our grades, teachers, homes, hairstyles, hair color, hair length, cars, jeans, shoes, presidents, scenery, weight, height, intelligence, perspective, situation, status, mood—we change, we change, we change! We're constantly changing.

Listen to what I've found: a human being loses an average of forty to one hundred strands of hair a day. Each square inch of a human body has an average of thirty-two million bacteria on it.

Talk about change.

Humans shed 600,000 particles of skin every hour, about one and a half pounds per year. By seventy years of age, an average person will have lost 105 pounds of skin. That's as much as some students weigh! Nerve impulses to and from the brain travel as fast as 170 mph. Your stomach needs to produce a new layer of mucus every two weeks, or it will digest itself. Your ears and nose continue to grow throughout your entire life. Fifteen million blood cells are destroyed by the human body every second.

There is change going on all the time. You're changing! You're changing! You're changing! And here's the problem: you can't control it. That's why some of you do some things that really harm your body, because you figure, "With everything changing around me, at least I can control myself."

Yet you can't get control, because change is happening all the time. That's why we talk about God's "immutability." He doesn't change.

You've probably heard about mutations. Mutations are the random genetic changes that produce new offspring. Something that is "mutable" is subject to change in any degree, therefore to be "immutable" means to be unchanging and unchangeable. That's what we mean about God.

Here are some interesting things to consider about God. Did you know God does not learn anything? To learn something means that He would change. He doesn't need to learn. He does not grow. He is never surprised. Isn't that an interesting thought? God is never surprised. You can't do something and have God go, "Wow, that surprised Me. I didn't know that."

God never improves. He is already one hundred percent God.

The word *always* can be used to express the truth of immutability. God is always wise. God is always in control. God is always fair. God is always good. He is always holy. He is always merciful. He always loves.

That's what we know about God: He never changes. We, on the other hand, do change and we need help understanding. So, when you're grappling with something you don't know and you're trying to find some answers, go to something that you do know. We know that God has the answers, and that He won't change on us.

Here's a statement I want you to think about as we talk about the immutability of God. Its author first started off by saying, "This is the most incredible statement on the immutability of God I've ever heard." When I first read it, I thought, "Really? Come on!" It really didn't hit me. It's one of those statements that as you think about it—in about two days you're going to go, "Wow, that's really cool." It sounds so simple. Are you ready? Here it is: *Nothing ever happens to God.* Nothing ever happens to God. It doesn't happen. Today things happened to you. The things you did and decisions you made were affected by outside forces or other people. You went to play basketball, you ate, you made decisions, but nothing happened to God, because God knows everything. He's immutable. No change is possible. In men, change is impossible to escape. But in God, change is totally impossible to happen.

The Bible talks a lot about God never changing.

Psalm 102:25-27 says:

"In the beginning you laid the foundations of the earth,
And the heavens are the work of Your hands.
They will perish, but you remain;
They will all wear out like a garment.
Like clothing you will change them and they will be discarded.
But You remain the same,
And your years will never end."

Malachi 3:6 says, "For I am the LORD, ***I do not change***; Therefore you are not consumed, O sons of Jacob."

Hebrews 6:17-18 says:

"So when God desired to show more convincingly to the heirs of the promise ***the unchangeable character of his purpose***, he guaranteed it with an oath, so that by two unchangeable things, in which it is impossible for God to lie, we who have fled for refuge might have strong encouragement to hold fast to the hope set before us" (ESV).

Aren't you glad for that? God has given both His promise and His oath. These are unchangeable because it is impossible for God to lie. Those of us who have experienced great pain because of a sudden or violent change in our lives can always rely on the character of God as an anchor. It never changes. There is hope in that stability.

James 1:17 says, "Every good gift and every perfect gift is from above, coming down from the Father of lights with ***whom there is no variation or shadow due to change"*** (ESV).

God doesn't cast a shadow as we would when we wait for the sun to change, for time to change, because God does not change. The passing of time doesn't affect Him.

Hebrews 1:12 says,

"Like a cloak You will fold them up,
And they will be changed.
But You are the same,
And Your years will not fail."

Hebrews 13:8 says, ***"Jesus Christ is the same yesterday, today, and forever."***

God never changes. God is immutable. God is the same. He never learns, He's always good, He's always holy, He's always just, He's always righteous. That is what we know about God.

You're saying, "All right, I get it—He doesn't change. But what about my hurt? What about these hard situations? If God is always holy, always just, then why did He let this happen?" How can we make God's immutability fit in with the messiness of everyday life? **How are we going to apply this to us?**

Here's some ways God's immutability helps us.

God's promises never change

God has made many promises to those who follow Him, and we can know these will never change. Ephesians 1:13 says, "In Him you also trusted, after you heard the word of truth, the gospel of your salvation; in whom also, having believed, you were sealed with the Holy Spirit of promise." God promises that, with the Holy Spirit, He will always be with you. James 1:12 says He promises life—an awesome, full, complete, total, out-of-this-world life: "Blessed is a man who endures tempation,; for when he has been approved, he will receive the crown of life, which the Lord has promised to those who love Him."

We're promised an abundant, awesome, incredible life—not in this world, but in the world to come. That's where we have to get our focus. There's an eternity out there. There's a forever out there. In that forever world, God says, "For those of you who persevere, for those of you who go after the crown of life, that go through the trials of this life, there's an awesome, full, complete, total, out-of-this-world life for you."

Not only that, but God's promises never change. In Titus 1:2, God promised a forever without pain, sorrow, sickness, and death. He says, "In hope of eternal life which God, who cannot lie, promised before time began." Everything that causes us to ask the "why" questions, God says, "I'm going to wipe that out, and that's a promise I will not change."

God's plan never changes

We change our plans all the time. Think about how many times today you changed your plans—because you were running late, or an unforeseen obstacle came up, or another person had a different plan. God doesn't have to deal with any of that. God says, "I never change my plan." Psalm 33:11 says, "The counsel of the LORD stands forever, the plans of His heart to all generations." Isaiah 14:24 says, "The LORD of hosts has sworn, saying, 'Surely, just as I have intended, so it has happened, and just as I have planned, so it will stand'" (NASB). Philippians 1:6 tells us, "Being confident of this very thing, that He who has begun a good work in you will complete it until the day of Jesus Christ."

God has a plan for your life. He created you. He saved you. He has a specific, detailed plan for your life, and that plan will not change.

When there is stress in your life, you know where it comes from? Stress is when there are two agendas. You know what that's like. Your mom or dad has an agenda and you don't like it. You know there's stress at home, right? God's got a plan for your life. You may say, "I don't know if I like that plan—I've got my own plan." Now, you can have a plan, but listen carefully: God's plan will not change. If you have stress in your life, it's probably because there are two plans. I suggest that you change your plan, because God's agenda is not going anywhere. God's plan—which is perfect for you, since He is God—never changes.

God's person never changes

A.W. Tozer said, "In coming to Him at any time, we need not wonder if we should find Him in a receptive mood. He is always receptive to misery and need as well as to love and faith. He does not keep office hours. Nor does He set aside periods where He will not see anybody. Nor does He change His mind about anything. Today, this moment, He feels towards His creatures, towards babies, towards sick, the fallen, the sinful exactly as He did when He sent

His only begotten Son into the world to die for mankind. God never changes His moods, or cools off His affections, or loses His enthusiasm."

You can go to God and not have to wonder if He's in a good mood. You know how sometimes you have to be careful going to your mom or dad, right? There are some times that you don't go to your mother or father because you know that if you ask them a question and they're not in a good mood, you're not going to get a good answer. God is never in a bad mood. He's never sad, never sick, never too busy. He's always there and He's always real. You can always go to Him.

God's passion never changes

John 6:37 says, "All that the Father gives Me will come to Me, and the one who comes to Me I will by no means cast out."

God says He will never, never reject one who comes to Him. God's passion never changes. His invitation is open. He says, "Look, I love you. I don't care how dirty, rotten, and filthy you are. My love is open for you to come. I want to forgive." The Bible talks a lot about God's love and grace, and we can know that not only will it not run out, be also that God is passionate—enthusiastic—about giving it to us. (The Bible also says those who reject Christ as their Savior will spend eternity in Hell; that will never change, either.)

Not only does God's passion about salvation never change, but God's passion also never changes concerning security. 2 Timothy 2:13 says, "If we are faithless [do not believe and are untrue to Him], He remains true [faithful to His Word and His righteous character], for He cannot deny Himself" (Amplified Version). Isn't that great? Even when we fail, even when we are foolish, God says, "I will not fail you. You have failed me, but I won't run away. I won't turn my back on you. I will be there for you." You've got security in a God who is passionately in love with you.

Knowing this about God doesn't necessarily change our response to Him, or our tough questions, though. **There are three things you can do with what we just said:**

1. You can compartmentalize.

You can suppress the truth. You may be reading this now and think, "I know that God is supposed to be immutable, but I think He changes His mind when it comes to this area in my life. I know God is right, and I know He is holy, just, loving, and kind, but when it comes to this problem in my life, He is obviously going to change His mind because He couldn't let this happen." You separate, or compartmentalize, what you have learned about God from the rest of the issues.

2. You can spiritualize it.

You can acknowledge the truth but not let it affect your life. You accept God's immutability as a fact, but your *understanding* of what happens doesn't necessarily help the pain. You think, "God never changes, He's holy and just—right, so just get over it." "So your mom and dad's marriage busted up, just get over it." "So you were molested when you were little, get over it." Just cram the Bible into your head and just deal with it!

Sorry, but that approach doesn't work for me.

3. You can internalize it.

What does this mean? Believe the truth. Not just hear it, or accept it, but believe it.

What's the truth? Here's the key: Right now, will you level with God? Will you tell Him how you really feel? Did you know that He's never threatened by honesty? Have you ever been honest with God about your hurt?

I was speaking to a Sunday school class of students once and asked, "Do you ever feel like God made a mistake?" They all responded with, "Yes." "Do you ever feel like God blew it?" "Yes." I turned to one young lady and asked her, "Did you ever tell God that?" She caught herself as she said, "Oh, no—I'd never tell God that!" I asked, "Why not?" She said, "Because I don't want God to know...what I'm...thinking."

God wants you to level with Him. Tell Him the truth. I'm not saying to throw up on Him and have a "get it off your chest" session. I'm saying pour out your heart to Him. Say, "God, where were You?" Pour it out! God is not threatened by honest questions. He wants you to know Him better, and the only way that will happen is if you communicate with Him. You are going to have to focus on the "Who," and not the "why," because God doesn't have to answer your "why" questions and often He doesn't.

There will be times in your life when you're going to have to say, "I don't understand, and I can't put it all together, but I know that God never changes; I know that God is immutable. I know that He's always holy, always just, always kind, always loving. I'm going to trust Him. I'm not going to trust in myself, in the questions I have." While we can't always get specific answers in this life, we can find comfort and hope in a God Who is in control of this life.

In the Book of Job, when terrible things happened to one of the strongest followers of God, Job kept asking why. At the end of the book, God said this: "Job, is it OK if I don't answer your why questions? I'll answer the why with Who. I am God. Is that OK with you?"

Let me share with you the rest of the story about Karen.

> *Right after it happened, I wondered, "Will I ever heal? Will the hurt ever go away? Would I ever understand why?" I had a million why questions. After twenty-seven years, God has never answered my question of why Karen committed suicide. But I did learn a lot about Who God is. God answered my "why" questions with "Who."*
>
> *I'm God, is that OK? Will you trust Me?*
>
> *I remember one of the first times I was able to share my tragic experience in public, and afterward a young lady came up to me with her fiancé. With tears in her eyes, she said, "You understand. Can you please talk to my fiancé? I didn't think anyone understood. I didn't think anyone went through what I went through." I began to see a small slice of why God allowed*

me to go through what I did. I was able to give hope, I was able to give understanding, I was able to share. I found it wasn't just me that went through this; there are thousands of us around the world that experience the same thing. Yet if we don't talk about it, we don't know. We feel isolated, but we are not. God never promised to take away the pain, crying, and hurt on this side of Heaven. But there is hope.

By the way, I met a beautiful young lady and fell in love, and she goes beyond all that I can imagine. She exceeded all my expectations. I thank God for her.

Chapter 3

Faithfulness

Mike Calhoun

When we experience pain in our lives, we all welcome a faithful friend who is willing to share our pain. Most of the people who minister to us in our dark times are not those who come to us quoting Christian clichés, but rather the ones who come simply to be with us.

In my darkest hour I vividly remember one of my friends saying to me, "I am not here to quote verses or give you instruction; I am here to just be with you." Those were some of the most comforting words I heard during that life crisis.

It is not that the Bible is not comforting, because God's Word does bring comfort and healing. But often well-meaning people are more prone to quote a Bible verse as a quick fix than to practice it.

Some situations have scarred and hurt us so deeply that words cannot even penetrate our pain. It takes time to process the things that hurt in order to understand and comprehend them. Thus the question, "Where was God when...?"

You may be thanking God that you have not experienced a crisis that has rocked your world—yet. But undoubtedly, many of you reading this book understand the depth of pain and sorrow. When in your life did you ask that question, "God, where were You?"

Maybe you have seen close friends go through hard times. Even if you have not experienced the death of a close friend or relative, you have still faced uncertainty or injustice. At some point in our lives, we will all be confronted with something so big and full of pain that we will find ourselves asking, "Where was God when...?"

In this chapter I want to try to help with that answer, but not with clichés or quick-fix formulas. At one of the most difficult times in my life, I came to realize that when my world fell apart, the only thing that was still true was what I knew about God.

I am being truthful with you when I say, "God is good," because He is. But that may not keep you from asking, "How can you say God is good when all this stuff is happening? Is God really in charge, because my world is crumbling!"

Christians are generally afraid to ask these tough questions. We are fearful that we will anger God, or that by asking these questions we may lose our faith. Some of us don't even want to hear others ask. It is easier to just pretend the questions will go away.

The reality is that most of us have asked these very same questions at a crisis point of our lives. Even if we're afraid to say them out loud, we've felt them in our hearts. What is the answer? What do we need to think about to help us know how to confront pain?

In this book we are examining the attributes of God in response to pain. Just as a reminder, an attribute is a way of referring to the characteristics of God—the qualities that make Him God. Considering some of the characteristics of God helps us understand more of what God is like and how He is acting in our lives.

The attributes of God not only tell us about Him but are also the answer to the question, "Where was God when...?" They will help us understand that God doesn't change, even when our circumstances are tough.

With that in mind, let's look at God's faithfulness. One of God's attributes is that He is faithful—not just some of the time, but always. The Word of God is very clear about His faithfulness to His children, but the reality we face every day leaves us with a lot of questions. If God is faithful, why did He forsake you, and why did He leave you alone? If He is faithful, why do bad things happen? If God is really faithful, why do you feel so insecure? If God is faithful, then why did He let you get raped? Why is your family struggling so hard with finances? If God is so faithful, why did He let your parents get a divorce?

These are tough questions that need real answers. I am not confronting you with these questions to discourage you, but rather to drive you to the Bible for the only true answer. The answer will only be found, my friend, in the person of God.

With that in mind, listen to the true story of a young man who came to the same place and was asking the same questions.

> *My dad left me when I was five. I know a lot of people can identify with my situation, of having your family basically fall apart. But sometimes I felt like no one understood. You see, my parents fought all the time. I remember one night in particular, when I stood behind the door with my ears covered as my mom and dad fought it out in the kitchen. Usually, it was just flying words, but that night my mom starting throwing dishes, too. When the third coffee mug broke against the wall, I just lost it. I said I would do anything for them to stop fighting. My dad looked at me like I've never seen him look before. He hugged me and explained to me that adults are bound to disagree sometimes. He used the "d" word for the first time—they promised they weren't going to get a divorce. I don't remember hearing that word before, but I got used to it soon. They did get a divorce. I remember that night, too. I grabbed onto my dad's leg and sat on his ankle, begging him not to go.*

You may have been there. You may even be there right now. You may have no clue what's going to happen at home. Or you're not sure who's going to be there in the future.

I don't say that to unnerve you—you're already unnerved. That's just the reality. You get around other people, and they're smiling and happy and everything seems to be fine, but you're going through incredibly difficult times in your life. You feel like you have to handle it all by yourself. But the truth of God's Word says something else.

What is the truth about God?

If we say God is faithful, what does that mean? It means that because God is unchanging, He cannot be unfaithful. He can't suddenly be unfaithful and still be God. If God forsakes you or leaves you, then He's not God, and He is not true to His Word.

Understand this: if He is not faithful, then He is not God. If He is not faithful here in the present, then our hope for the future is in question. As a believer, He has promised you a place in Heaven, but if He is unfaithful now, then that is not very reassuring for the future.

But He is God, and He is faithful. He is always true to His promises. You may not feel like this is true right now, but based upon the truth of the Bible, you and I can rest in His promises.

Here's another way of saying God is faithful: He is dependable. Have you ever had a friend let you down? Are you thinking of that friend who said, "Yeah, I'm right there with you. I won't let you down," but then they left you when you needed them?

God is loyal. That's what it means to say that He is faithful.

Another way of saying it is to say that He is stable and unwavering. You've got friends that are up one day and down the next day—one day they like you, and the next day they don't; one day they talk to you, the next day they don't. Not God—God is faithful.

God will never be inconsistent. You'll never see Him contradict Himself, because He is faithful. All of His actions—everything that God does—are based on the fact that He is faithful.

I understanding that as you read this, you may be questioning if I really know what I'm talking about. This is a lot of information; I'm trying to lay some groundwork for you. But I want you to understand that I'm not just unpacking this information. I am not simply looking for you to respond like a child, repeating what a parent just said to them.

Right now, you just don't feel like God is faithful. But one of the things we all have to learn in our Christian walk is to separate feelings from fact. We must never let our feelings override the truth of the Word of God.

I am not suggesting that we become stoic and push our feelings aside. Very simply, we cannot let our feelings *guide* us. When our world falls apart, we have to come back to the One Who does not change. God is faithful and does not change, even when our feelings are erratic.

So, even as we deal with our feelings, let's look at the facts: What does the Bible say about this?

> Deuteronomy 7:9: "Therefore know that the LORD your God, He is God, the faithful God who keeps covenant and mercy for a thousand generations with those who love Him and keep His commandments."

> Psalm 9:10: "And those who know Your name will put their trust in You; for You, LORD, have not forsaken those who seek You."

> Psalm 89:8: "O LORD God of hosts, who is mighty like You, O LORD? Your faithfulness also surrounds You."

When I read about God and how good He is, it is tough for me to understand why God would have ever saved me in the first place. I really don't understand it. There's nothing special about me, so why would He love me enough to die for me and take my sin? Why would He do this?

You know what's even tougher for me to try to grab a hold of? After being a Christian all these years, I really don't understand why He still puts up with me. After all He has done for me, I still make sinful decisions, still am unfaithful to Him. Yet He continues to love me. I feel like I'm in the remedial class spiritually. But He never gives up on me. He is always faithful.

> Psalm 94:14: "For the LORD will not cast off His people, nor will He forsake His inheritance."

> Psalm 119:90: "Your faithfulness endures to all generations; You established the earth, and it abides."

> Psalm 121:3-4: "He will not allow your foot to be moved; He who keeps you will not slumber. Behold, He who keeps Israel shall neither slumber nor sleep."

He doesn't sleep. He's not going to fall asleep and leave you somewhere.

> Lamentations 3:22-23: "Through the LORD's mercies we are not consumed, because His compassions fail not. They are new every morning; great is Your faithfulness."

> Romans 3:3-4: "For what if some did not believe? Will their unbelief make the faithfulness of God without effect? Certainly not! Indeed, let God be true but every man a liar. As it is written: 'That You may be justified in Your words, and may overcome when You are judged.'"

Here's the idea of Romans 3:3-4: Paul asks, "If the people do not believe God is faithful, does that make Him unfaithful?" I love the way Paul answers when he says, "No way, this does not change a thing." Now, that's my translation. Paul actually says "certainly not" or "definitely not," depending on which translation you read. The bottom line is that just because you don't believe it, that doesn't make it true and doesn't change it. God is still faithful!

> 1 Corinthians 1:9: "God is faithful, by whom you were called into the fellowship of His Son, Jesus Christ our Lord."

> 1 Corinthians 10:13: "No temptation has overtaken you except such as is common to man; but God is faithful, who will not allow you to be tempted beyond what you are able, but with the temptation will also make the way of escape, that you may be able to bear it."

> 1 Thessalonians 5:24: "He who calls you is faithful, who also will do it."

Titus 1:2: "In hope of eternal life which God, who cannot lie, promised before time began."

Hebrews 10:23: "Let us hold fast the confession of our hope without wavering, for He who promised is faithful."

When you are in these difficult times, hang on to what you know. Don't worry about the things you don't know; hang on to what you do know, because God is faithful.

1 John 1:9: "If we confess our sins, He is faithful and just to forgive us our sins and to cleanse us from all unrighteousness."

This is an incredible verse for those of us who do know Christ as Savior. Even though we may struggle to give God everything, and even though we often rebel, He is still faithful. When we sin, if we confess our sin, He is faithful and just, and He will forgive us and cleanse us. God is a God of the second chance. You know why? Because He is faithful.

This is a lot of great information, but maybe you're wondering, "OK, so how does this really apply to me?" Where does God's faithfulness start to affect your life? We need to understand that God's faithfulness is the source of several components of our faith.

For example:

His faithfulness is the source of our deliverance from temptation. Remember 1 Corinthians 10:13? If God is not faithful, then you have no hope of overcoming sin and temptation. You may be struggling right now with some sin that has enslaved you, wondering if there is hope.

Maybe you are enslaved by pornography, eating disorders, or a multitude of other issues. You feel engulfed and wonder if there is help. I want you to understand that God can help you, and in Him is hope for overcoming our bondage to sin. He has promised that in every situation, He will faithfully be there to make a way to escape temptation. God can help because He is faithful.

Because He is faithful, He is the source of our assurance of our salvation. If God is not faithful, then there is no assurance of salvation. But because He is faithful, He is our security. We can trust in Him. We know that we can have forgiveness of sin.

Because of His security, we can have a foundation for ministry. In 2 Corinthians 1:18, the Apostle Paul attributes the whole foundation of his ministry to this fact. He says, "I can have this ministry because God is faithful." Without a faithful God, ministry would change because it would be based on something that was always changing.

Because God is faithful, He is the source of the challenge to righteous living. Since God is faithful to us, we are challenged to live a righteous life.

> 1 Peter 4:19: "Therefore let those who suffer according to the will of God commit their souls to Him in doing good, as to a faithful Creator."

Peter writes, "Look, I want to encourage you, so that when you're going through hard times, you understand that God is still faithful, and that faithfulness can motivate you to righteous living." God's faithfulness calls us to be faithful back to Him.

God is faithful in spite of our faithlessness. Songwriter and musician Jeremy Camp has experienced crisis in his life. He was a newly married young man, four months into marriage, when his wife died. Now, humanly speaking, that just doesn't make sense. He says that as he was processing this great loss, he struggled to even read his Bible.

Some may gasp and say, "I can't believe he said that." But if you have ever been in one of those dark tunnels of life, you can understand it better. This is not to minimize the importance of the Bible; it's just that the pain is so deep that nothing makes sense, not even the one thing that is true.

Because God is faithful, He always demonstrates His steadfast love. God always shows love, even when we aren't loveable. There are many times when I look at my life and I think, "If I were God, I would zap me." You might be laughing, but understand something: before I zapped me, I'd zap you. You're just as bad!

But God's love is steadfast, never changing. Isn't that amazing?

God's faithfulness is most greatly seen in the work of His Son, Jesus Christ. The fact that Jesus Christ loved us, died for us, paid the price for our sin, and rose again is evidence of His faithfulness. The reason we have salvation is because of God's faithfulness.

God's loyal love knows no limits. Have you ever thought about one of your friends and said, "If they do this one more time, that's it, we're done." You probably know someone just like that. Here's one of the incredible truths about God's faithfulness: you will never push God past His limits. You will never do anything to cause Him to be unfaithful to you.

We all know that people lie and sometimes break their word. But God does neither. He never lies, and He never breaks His word to us.

I think we need to rejoice in God's faithfulness. I think we need to get to the point where we can celebrate His faithfulness, even in hard times.

If you read the Book of Joshua, you'll find a reference in a couple of passages to the children of Israel crossing the Jordan River. Part of the process of making this miraculous crossing, made possible only by God, was the building of two memorials. The memorials were the Israelites' celebration of God's faithfulness.

God had led them out of Egypt and through the Red Sea, but now they would see whether He was faithful to deliver them again. He did it again. He performed a miracle and parted the water so they could walk on dry ground, they celebrated. They were facing the impossible, but God was faithful to do what they were not capable of doing.

The great thing is that they built two memorials, and one was in the middle of the river bed. They were celebrating God's faithfulness in the middle of pressure and difficulty.

When we see God's faithfulness in our pain, we should celebrate, too.

If you are still in the dark place, will you accept and believe that God doesn't change—that He is faithful? Maybe you can say, "God, I don't know what You are doing to me. I don't know why You are letting my parents get divorced. I don't know why You let this happen to me—I don't know why. I don't know why, but I still believe."

The challenge is to walk by faith even when we don't know why. Can you celebrate the fact that you believe God is faithful when you are in the dark place? Crisis will not make you a person of faith; it will reveal whether or not you are a person of faith.

Look at what Job said and remember that this is a man who went through pain beyond description. Yet he says, "Even though He kills me, I will still serve Him." Now there's a man who knew how to praise God and celebrate His faithfulness in the hard times.

There's one more step in the process. Now that we know what God's faithfulness is—we have seen what the Bible says and how it says this understanding should show up in our lives—what are we going to do with the truth? Maybe you looked at the statement, "Crisis will not make you a person of faith; it will reveal whether or not you are a person of faith," and said, "Whew, I'm in crisis, but I certainly don't feel like a person of faith. This has been really hard, but I do want to trust God's faithfulness. How can I make this truth part of my life?"

There are three things you can do with this truth about God.

1. You can compartmentalize it.

You can suppress the truth. This means you choose to disregard it. We try to just fit God into our little, mixed-up world. But here's the problem with attempting to fit God into our problem: we are finite (limited), and God is infinite (unlimited).

God is without limit and our worlds are so small. It's like having a small shirt and trying to fit it on an extra large man. It just doesn't work.

Here's what we try to do when we try to compartmentalize God. We say, "OK, God, I know You are big, but guess what,

I don't believe You are always faithful. I'm still not sure You are dependable. After all, I see all the problems and pressures of the world, and it just doesn't make sense. I think You are inconsistent."

What we have to do is change our focus. The past is painful, the present is overwhelming, and the future is just so uncertain, but the only way to change is if you change your focus by looking at God. We cannot fit this infinite, faithful God into our understanding of life. Trying to do that is compartmentalizing and ignoring the truth.

2. You can spiritualize.

This means you acknowledge the truth. This is where you buy into some of the Christian clichés. You accept it with your head, but not with your heart. "God is always faithful." "God never fails." "God never lets me down." It's all in your head, but you have not applied it to your heart. You say these things over and over, but inside you're still in turmoil, and you're just barely hanging on in these moments of crisis.

When we just buy into the clichés, we do so blindly. We do not take the time to search the Scriptures for truth; we simply quote someone else. When people try to encourage you in your pain and tell you God is faithful, you acknowledge it in your head while knowing it is unsettled in your heart.

In order to make application of this truth and to ingrain it into your life, you will need to go beyond what others say. It will mean personally going to the Word of God to search out the answer. Then and only then will you be able to say with conviction from your heart, "God is faithful; I know it and believe it." You should not be content just to parrot what others say.

So what is the answer? What is the right way to approach truth? Let's look at the third response you can have to truth.

3. You can internalize it.

This means you believe the truth. This is the point of believing God's character.

It seems that people are willing to believe anybody but God. In the world of finance, people are often swindled out of millions of dollars because they believe the investor. The very same people that trust someone with a million or a billion dollars are the very same people who would say they couldn't trust God. What we have to do is come to the place where we acknowledge and internalize the truth, saying, "I'm going to trust God even if I don't understand."

Remember the young man at the beginning of this chapter who talked about divorce? I want you to read a little bit more of his story.

My dad did it. He left. He abandoned me.

I never took the church and God thing seriously. It just seemed fake whenever I tried to believe it in reality. Heavenly Father? If He's anything like my real father, I don't want anything to do with Him. Ever since my dad left, I just thought everyone would start abandoning me.

I started writing sometime in middle school. I guess you could say all that resentment inside of me turned out to be something good. I won a few awards and I even had a piece published.

I got a letter last week from the magazine where my column was published. It was a bunch of Scripture verses put into a letter, trying to express how God felt about me.

It said, "I've been misrepresented by those who do not know Me. I am not distant and angry, but in the complete expression of love, it is My desire to lavish My love on you simply because you are My child and I am your Father. I care for you more than your earthly father ever could, for I am the perfect Father. One day I will wipe every tear from your eyes, and I will take away all the pain you have suffered on this earth. I am your Father and I love you, even as I love My Son Jesus."

Like I said, it's making me think.

"I've been misrepresented by those who do not know Me."

Perhaps you can identify in that you realize God has been misrepresented even in your own life. You haven't taken the step to really believe what God says about Himself and how that will change your life; instead you're content to let the clichés fail you. Why not take a step into belief and embrace God's faithfulness?

Chapter 4

Sovereignty

Ric Garland

If you are honest with yourself, sometimes you feel God is not really there. He doesn't feel real to you sometimes.

You may be thinking, "Don't say those things. You can think them, but you can't say them." Well, I want to talk about these things that maybe you're thinking but haven't ever told anyone else or dealt with yourself. You're probably coming from one of two places.

1. You have not received Jesus Christ as your Savior. You may be thinking, "I do believe there is a God, but I can't trust Him. Something bad happened in my life and it's just too hard to let God be in control. If I can't trust Him to take care of my life right now, why should I trust Him for what comes after this life?"

2. You may know Jesus Christ as your personal Savior. You put your trust in Him to save you, but you're not sure you trust Him any more than that. You may be thinking, "I'm not sure I want to give my all. To be honest with you, my life really stinks. There have been things that have happened in my life that I'm not really sure why God let them happen. I'm OK with trusting Him to save

me, but I've got to look out for myself, because I'm not sure He knows, or cares, about what I'm going through."

These two attitudes go back to whether you can really trust God, a deep question you may be afraid to answer. Think about the hard situations you've experienced, and some of the questions you've had for God, and see if you've been wondering whether you can trust Him.

When we think about whether we can really trust God, we need to go back to what we believe about God. The attribute we're going to talk about in this chapter, **sovereignty**, is one of the most important truths we know about God.

As you think about whether you truly trust God, ask yourself what you believe about what the Bible says about His sovereignty.

Here's the concept behind sovereignty: God is in control. He has total control of this world. I know what you're thinking: "Wait a minute, if God is in control, then why does all this bad stuff happen?" Did God let the tsunami happen in Southeast Asia? If God is in total control of this universe, did He just stand by and watch over 200,000 people die? Why does He allow a child to be molested?

Let's make it personal. Why did He allow you to be molested? If God is in control, why did He allow you to feel this pain so bad inside that you keep it hidden and can't talk about it? If God is in control, why did He allow your friend to die? If God is in control, why did He allow your parents to get a divorce? If God is all-powerful, if He can do whatever He pleases and has complete control over this universe, then why does He allow these things to happen?

It doesn't make sense. We may make feeble attempts to explain it—God did it because of this, or He meant this—but really, we can't figure it out. It totally doesn't fit that a God Who's completely in control would let all this hurt happen.

Let me share the story of a student at the Bible Institute, his situation and his questions.

I have a twin brother. Two weeks after I left for college, God tried to take him away from me. He let his car spin out onto the highway, right into a tractor trailer. My brother laid there in the car, trapped under the trailer, crumpled up like a piece of paper, for an hour. God let my parents wonder if they still had two children. He made me regret leaving for college, leaving my family. God let my brother go through surgeries, tests, scans, pills, and hospitals. God let us wonder if our dream of opening a theater would ever come true. Then, my brother started to recover, and God let us think everything would be all right. He let us think that the bones would heal, and that our dream was still possible. But then God let a bump grow right in the midst of it all—a tumor God had been hiding from us—on the left side of his brain. Soon he'll have to go into the hospital, get sliced open, have metal replace bone. Why would He put us through all this just to make my brother suffer more? Why would He wait to take him now? God had His chance to take my brother in that car accident. God can't change His mind now.

Here's a real-life experience of someone going through tough times. This student is not only having to deal with his own pain, but he's also watching his parents and brother suffer. And on top of it all, he has to deal with this pain even though he has a personal relationship with the God of the universe, Who's supposed to be in control.

I remember going into a cancer hospital to visit some friends and their daughter who was sick. My wife and I passed by a room with a mom sitting next to the bed of a three-month-old baby with cancer. How do you tell a mom who's sitting next to a three-month-old baby with cancer, "Don't worry. God's in control." How do you say that?

I want you to understand that this is real. I believe that the Bible is a real book, and it talks about real issues. I don't want to demean anything that you are going through. It's tough; it really is. But I think that sometimes we turn away from hard issues because we don't know how to deal with them, and it only gets harder for us. God is not afraid of the hard issues or the hard questions.

Let's look at the truth about God. What does it mean that God is sovereign?

Sovereign means *supreme authority*. To be a sovereign means you have supreme authority over something, or in this case, that God is the Supreme Being over the entire universe.

Now, God is supreme and in control, but at the same time, we are free to make our own choices. Here's where it gets a little technical—stay with me. Sovereignty and freedom form an antinomy. An antinomy is when you have two truths that cannot be true at the same time, but they are. For example, Jesus Christ is one hundred percent God and one hundred percent man. That's impossible by our technical definitions, but it's true. Here we have another antinomy. God is all-powerful and He is in complete and total control. But on the same side, God also allows for freedom.

Someone said it this way, "God controls everything that is consistent in His decrees. Therefore, while sovereign, He does not violate the free will of man." He lovingly allows us to make our own decisions. Some of you are saying, "Well, if God controls everything, then why do I make any choices? Why do I have to get saved? If He's got it all figured out anyways, why do I have to deal with Him? God knows everything."

Here's a statement that may frustrate you, but here goes anyway. God not only chose who would be saved, but also the way they would be saved—through their own free will. You see, people go to Hell because they reject God's truth by choosing to live by their own truth instead. It's their choice. People go to Heaven, however, because of God's grace, not because they are better than anyone else. So in God's sovereign control, He's allowed—He's decreed—the fact that we have free choice. God allows us to make choices and we are responsible for those choices that we make.

Now let's look at some Scripture verses that talk about God's sovereignty.

> Isaiah 46:9-11: "Remember the former things of old,
> For I am God, and there is no other;
> I am God, and there is none like Me,
> Declaring the end from the beginning,
> And from ancient times things that are not yet done,
> Saying, 'My counsel shall stand,

And I will do all My pleasure,'
Calling a bird of prey from the east,
The man who executes My counsel, from a far country.
Indeed I have spoken it;
I will also bring it to pass.
I have purposed it;
I will also do it."

Ephesians 1:11: "In Him also we have obtained an inheritance, being predestined according to the purpose of Him who works all things according to the counsel of His will."

Psalm 135:6: "Whatever the LORD pleases He does,
In heaven and in earth,
In the seas and in all deep places."

These verses explain that not only is God supreme over everything, but He can do what He pleases since He is God.

1 Chronicles 29:12: "Both riches and honor come from You, and You reign over all. In Your hand is power and might; in Your hand it is to make great and to give strength to all."

Revelation 22:13: "I am the Alpha and the Omega, the Beginning and the End, the First and the Last."

Alpha and Omega are the first and last letters in the Greek alphabet. It's like saying, "I'm A to Z. I'm everything. I'm totally comprehensive. I am God."

Isaiah 45:5-6: "I am the LORD, and there is no other;
There is no God besides Me.
I will gird you, though you have not known Me,
That they may know from the rising of the sun to its setting
That there is none besides Me.
I am the LORD, and there is no other."

There are a lot of people who say they are their own god, and there are others who believe in other gods, but God says there's only one God out there. He says, "I am the Lord. There is no one besides me. No one competes with me. No one could even come up to me because

I am God. I make plans. I have a plan, and it's not going to change. Nobody can shove it out of the way. No one can move it, because I have the power of the entire world. I am in control."

Another way of saying it is this: God is in control; He has the absolute right to do anything according to what He wants. That's God. God is totally, absolutely in control.

You ask, "How does that apply to my situation? Does He not care? Is He OK with my parents getting divorced? Did He want me to be molested? Does He want people I love to suffer, and have me watch them suffer?" Think about the young man who shared the story earlier: "I'm trying to go to college, even Bible college, and to do right for God, and my twin brother gets in an accident. He could have died, and now we're all excited because he's healing, and then we find out he's got a bump inside, and it's growing, and it's cancer." God, why do You seem to torture people?

How do we apply this to our situations? Remember what we talked about at the beginning of the chapter—those questions deep inside that we don't often say out loud? They all came back to one main question: Can I trust God? Or really, can I trust God when I can't understand? That's the main problem here: we can't understand. We can't figure out how His goodness and sovereignty fit together, or how bad situations happen when He loves us.

Rabbi Harold S. Kushner wrote a book called *When Bad Things Happen to Good People*. Here's what he says: "We feel we need to make a choice between a good God Who is not totally powerful and a powerful God Who is not totally good." In his book, he chooses a good God Who is not always powerful.

Can we do the same thing? Can we say, "This God we trust in, the God of the Bible, is good, but He's not totally powerful"? Rabbi Kushner is saying the same thing the student said in his story earlier: "Look, if God is all-powerful and He lets bad things happen, then He's not good. But yet if He's all-good, then He's not all-powerful, because He wouldn't let this pain happen." It can't be both. How do you answer something like that? What do you tell yourself as you deal with these hard situations—are you going to have to accept that your

God is either not powerful or not good?

Where we're stuck is that we are trying to define a holy, infinite God by human, finite measures. Like I said before, the main question is whether we trust God when we can't understand. That's why we question God's sovereignty—because it doesn't add up for us.

When we don't understand other people, our first response is usually to judge. It's not a stretch to think that maybe we do that to God, too. He knows what He's doing, but as we see different events unfold, we get scared and think that what we know about Him may have changed. We try to trust what we see from God rather than just trusting God.

So, one way to deal with these hard situations is to realize we don't understand, and to accept that God knows all of what is going on while we only know part of it. But some pretty terrible stuff still happens—what about that? What does that mean?

This is where God's *sovereignty* is especially reassuring. Not only does He know what is happening, but He has power over it, too. We can trust that God is not only good, and making the best choice that is best for us, but we can also trust that He is *completely* powerful and sovereign. If there is a single event in the entire universe that can happen outside of God's sovereign control, then we could not trust Him. (We can still obey Him, though—we obey many people in our lives who have authority over us, even if we don't think we can trust them. When God says, "Don't steal," we can obey Him, but that's different than trying to trust Him when your parents get divorced. So, the question here is not whether you are obeying God's commandments, but whether you are trusting Him and allowing that to affect your life.) There is no way I am going to trust a God that is not in control of everything. So, to be "God," He must be sovereign—in complete control.

Here's what I found out. In order to trust God, we must always view our adverse circumstances through the eyes of faith—in what God says is true—and not sense. It doesn't matter what you see or feel. Your senses can betray you. I've heard that the airline pilots have to rely on their instruments when flying an airplane. Why? Because their senses can betray them. You and I know that in our own lives. Sometimes our senses betray us and we've got to say, "I don't understand this. My world is rocked and it's spinning. But I've got to trust God even when it doesn't make sense to me."

God is in control. He has told us that and wants us to believe it even if our circumstances look different.

After reading these verses and hearing these truths, you may be ready to say, "OK, God is sovereign and God is good. He loves me and is totally in control. I can trust Him. But where does the pain come from? Why does He let us hurt?" Why? Well, the Bible tells us some things about the effects of sin or how God wants us to grow through trials, but the bottom line is, I don't know. I don't know why God lets us experience pain. I do know this: in the midst of our suffering, we must believe that God is in control and that He is sovereign. Also, that somehow, someway, somewhere, what God is allowing us to go through is going to be for His glory and our good.

Here's our problem. We are very human-centric. We're always stuck on how our circumstances are affecting us. That's our greatest weakness. But what about being God-centric—"God, how can this be used for Your glory?"

I love this statement: **God never wastes pain**. I don't know what kind of pain you are going through in your life. I don't know the depth of some of the things you are going through. I can tell you this: if your God is sovereign, and your God has complete control of everything, then even the depth of the pain that you're experiencing will not be wasted by God.

Nothing is so trivial or small to escape the attention of God's sovereign control, and nothing is so great to be beyond His power to control it. God is interested in both the small and great things of life, from a student being bullied to the people who live where the tsunami landed in Asia. He thinks about the birds of the field as much as big, powerful governments. He cares about something as trivial as whether you pass or fail a test, or something important, like in what direction your life is headed. Both sides! God cares! He cares!

I love this: in his book *Trusting God*, Jerry Bridges says, "Neither the willful, malicious acts nor the unintended mistakes of man's will can thwart God's purpose for us." Isn't that great? There is nothing on this earth that can thwart God's will for your life. You might think, "If that guy didn't abuse me." "If this girl didn't do this to me." "If this incident didn't happen to me." "If I wasn't wrongfully accused." "If this didn't happen, then things would be different." No! God, Who has control over everything, says, "No one can thwart My plan."

God never makes mistakes and He never has any regrets. So we know His plan and purpose for us are perfect. We know that He also has the power to carry it out. Nothing happens that cannot be used for God's glory and our good. Nothing. Forget what it is that you are struggling with. Forget the depth of the pain or how you're feeling. Let me just say it clearly: God can use everything, everything for His glory and your good. Even your sin? Yes! God can use the stupid attacks of your life. He can use the wicked things and turn them around. If only you're willing to yield, surrender, and trust Him. That's what it all comes back to—trusting God. He can use the pain. He can use it for His glory and for your good.

So how are you going to process this in your life? We just went over some pretty intense things. How are you going to process this? How is this going to flesh out in your life? There are three things you can do.

1. You can compartmentalize it.

This means that you suppress the truth. You can say something like, "Hey, God was not in control when this painful situation happened. He is a good, but He can't be completely powerful if this happened." If you think about it, this may be how you practically believe. You may say that you're saved and that you believe the Bible, but your heart doesn't totally believe what God has said about Him being both good and in control. You don't trust Him. You're saying, "God let it happen, so obviously I'm not saying He's an evil God or a bad God. I'm saying He is good, but maybe there's some stuff He can't stop." If you're being honest, that's where you are. You're compartmentalizing that part of God out of your mind. His sovereignty isn't part of what you really believe about Him.

2. You can spiritualize.

This means you can acknowledge the truth, but you really don't bring it home. You can say something like, "I don't totally understand God's sovereignty and how that fits in with the choices I make or the pain I feel, but I'm going to try to figure it out. I'm going to study God's sovereignty and I'm going to analyze this situation, and I'm going to figure out how it all fits together and why God would do this." But you're missing the point: God wants you to trust Him. He asks you to believe what He has told you about Himself, not become all-knowing. You can have a good understanding of what the Bible says, but that understanding is meant to help you know God better, not figure out why life happens the way it does.

Here's my recommendation.

3. You can internalize the truth—really believe it.

Trusting God in the midst of the pain and the heartache means we accept it from Him. Now, this is tough. Trusting God in the midst of our pain and our heartache means that we *accept it from Him*. Did you get that? God's allowing this to happen. We can't figure it out. We don't know why. It doesn't make sense to us. But we *accept* that it is from God.

Here's an important concept I really want you to get: **There's a big difference between acceptance and resignation or submission.**

Have you ever watched extreme fighting? A word they use is *submission*. That's when one guy overpowers the other one. For you to submit to somebody means that somebody overpowers you, somebody has more authority over you, or you fear the consequences if you don't give in. And so some of us say, "Well, I know I've got to submit to God. God's more powerful than I am. I might as well submit to Him." Or, "I'll resign. I'm tired of fighting. I know I can't win. I'll just give up." That is not what God is looking for. If He wanted to force you into submission or resignation, He could. But He wants you to accept the truth.

Internalizing the truth is saying, "God, I'm not just going to submit to You. I'm not just going to resign to You. God, I don't know why this happened. I don't know why this is happening. I don't know why You're allowing me to grow through this. It makes no sense to me. But God, I will acknowledge that You are in total control, and because of that, I will accept it."

This is not easy. You don't say a phrase three times and click your heels and you'll be in Kansas. It's not just verbally saying it. It's getting to the core of your heart and saying, "God, I've got to accept this even though I don't understand." Trusting God is not a matter of how you feel. It's a matter of your will. It's making a choice, even when you don't feel like it!

Can I be honest with you? There are times when I don't feel like God is making the right choices. There are things in my life that I am still questioning why God allowed them to happen to me. But trusting Him isn't about how I feel. Even though I feel those things, I say, "God, I am going to choose to trust You anyway." My act of the will must be based on belief—trusting Him—and that belief must be based on the truth that He's given me.

That's why we go back to the Bible. That's why we read the Scriptures. That's why we cling to these truths even though it doesn't make sense. Why? Because nothing happens that cannot be used for God's glory and for my good. Nothing, nothing, NOTHING!

Remember the young man's whose brother got in an accident and then found the bump? Let's hear some more of the story.

> *I just needed someone to blame for everything that had happened. It was really no one's fault that my brother was in the accident, enduring all that pain, enduring all those injuries just to find out about the tumor. I couldn't blame my brother. I couldn't blame the other drivers, really. God was just a target of opportunity. Now that I look back on it all, it's all about perspective. When things seem to go my way, it's easier to believe that God is love. But it's not easy when the whole world is falling apart. What I've learned through these things is that when I put my whole focus on those things that are happening around me,*

it's harder to believe that the God I know would allow this. He has always been there for me, but it's hard to believe when all I can see is pain. The same thing can go in the other direction. When I focus on the Savior, it doesn't take the pain away, it just makes it easier to believe the truth. An old hymn I used to sing is:

"Turn your eyes upon Jesus.
Look full in His wonderful face.
And the things of earth will grow strangely dim,
In the light of His glory and grace."

How much of the pain you're dealing with is because your focus is on the suffering and not what you know is true about God? How often do you stop and reflect on truths about God and what He has done in your life?

Remember Job? The book starts out with God asking Satan a question. Satan "takes advantage" of the situation to challenge God's way with men, and God allows Satan to cause suffering in the life of Job. Job's three friends try to "counsel" Job, coming to the conclusion that Job must have sinned.

I believe that the Book of Job was not written to Satan, but for us. It's meant to keep our focus and our trust on the holy, sovereign God Who does not owe us an explanation.

God will never answer all of our "why" question. But in the midst of the "why," He answers with "Who." He is there. He is in control—even when I don't understand. Is that OK?

The Book of Job does not conclude with a conversation between God and Satan in which God claims victory over Satan.

Rather, it concludes with a conversation between God and Job in which Job acknowledges that through his trials, he has come into a new and deeper relationship with God.

God gave Job "Who" instead of "why." Is that enough for you?

Chapter 5

God's Love

Mike Calhoun

Have you ever felt like you cried out to God and nothing happened? Like He wasn't there? When it comes to the topic of "Where Was God?" the easy part is asking the hard questions. Life is so riddled with pain that it is not difficult to "knock the scab off of the sore."

But once we have opened the wound, then what do we do? How do we answer the hard questions without being trite? Perhaps you have never entertained the question of, "Where was God when...?" because you were ashamed to admit that you could not connect the dots in your life.

I can tell you that you're not alone. This question, or at least some variation of it, is more common than we think. Maybe these exact words are not the ones silently screamed in the night; sometimes it's just "Why?"

When I began working with students, I watched as they dealt with hardship and pain. They were faced with tragedy then, but over the years students' lives seem to have become more complicated. The pain has intensified. Perhaps the reason why is because someone can die in an entirely different country and we can know about it within minutes. Media and the Internet have brought the world's pain up close and personal. Students today are just overwhelmed.

So, where was God? Where was He when that terrible thing happened in your life? You have heard others ask the same question: "If God is good, then why did He let this happen?" I read one blog that said, speaking sarcastically about God and crisis, "Hey, He did let this tragedy happen on His watch—maybe He doesn't care."

You may struggle with hearing these questions—just thinking someone would be so bold as to say this out loud. How could somebody question God like that? How could someone accuse God of not caring? In Christianity we've tried to neatly package everything. We don't ask the hard questions. We prefer to just put the blinders on, quote the verses that make us feel good, and hope that everything will be OK. The problem, though, is that we are living in a real world and everything is not always OK.

So, is there an answer to this question? Yes, I believe there is. Let me put it this way:

1. If I didn't believe there was an answer to this question, then I would not be writing this book. I have no desire to spread propaganda; I want to speak truth that affects you at the core of your being.

2. If I didn't believe there was an answer to this question, then I would not be in youth ministry.

3. If I didn't believe there was an answer to this question, then I would not even be a Christian myself.

But there is an answer and we are going to discover it together.

The simple answer is that God is good and everything is going to work out. You may not see it in your lifetime, but that doesn't change the truth.

That's the simple answer, but behind that simple answer are some very complex truths. In order to discover those truths, we must look at the only constant in life: God. God is not just the Christian answer, He is *the* answer. This is not a Christian slogan; it is fact. All of us either have come or will come to the day when we have to realize that the answer to "why" is "Who."

I can tell you when I came to that day in my life. It was the day I realized my whole world had fallen apart and nothing made sense. All of the "spiritual" answers left me feeling empty. There seemed to be no real answers. I didn't know what to do. Have you ever been there?

The answer is not, "OK, everything is going to work out and God is good." The real answer is just this: God.

Let's continue our study of the attributes, or characteristics, of God. The attribute we want to look at in this chapter is that God is love.

This is probably one of the most well-known concepts about God. You have heard people talk about God's love or that God is love, but what does that really mean? Generally speaking, when most people refer to the love of God they see it as an emotion rather than an attribute. But God's love is not based on emotion. God does not just love; He *is* love.

God is love

Simply viewing God's love as an emotion will leave you still dealing with your questions. You will find yourself still asking, "Why did this happen? If God really is the God of love and truly loves me, then why do I get mistreated by people?"

If God's love is just an emotion, you will continue to ask, "If God really loves me, why am I feeling like an outcast in my own youth group? If God really loves me, then why did I study but still flunk in school? If God really loves me, then why did He let my brother die? If God really loves me, then why did He let me get abused? If God really loves me, then why do I not have a best friend? If God really loves me, then why doesn't He take away my mother's anger? Why does He let her hurt me?" Hard questions, right?

With these questions, the "everything is OK" answer is not enough. Although we'd like to assume that everything will work out if we love Jesus, thinking that will only disillusion us. Reality shows us a different picture.

Reality is that real people who love a real God with all their heart still have real problems. They experience pain just like those who do not love Jesus. The difference is that believers have a foundation for a different kind of life, a life found in God.

Listen to the real-life story of a young lady named Jen who has been devastated by the loss of her fiancé.

> *I was only twenty years old when I watched the love of my life slip away. Josh was twenty-three. He loved God. We were engaged and deeply in love. He wanted to marry me and then we planned to serve God in youth ministry.*
>
> *So why would God allow Josh to be diagnosed with such a rare form of leukemia that even the best hospitals had no treatment for the cancer? I watched as Josh lived through chemo treatments and was so sick he couldn't even talk to me.*
>
> *We had hundreds and even thousands of people praying for Josh's healing. I thought for sure God would let him live, but God didn't answer our prayers for healing. I sat with Josh for the last ten days of his life and watched the cancer literally eat away at him. Was this my Josh? Was this person laying in this hospital bed the same guy who loved me and with whom I had planned on serving God? Why would God let His faithful young follower suffer in such a way?*
>
> *After a year of struggling, Josh passed away. I felt as though part of me died along with him. How could I go on? What was I going to do? My life with Josh was going to be so amazing. We were two young people who loved God and were serving Him with our lives. Being with Josh was going to be my greatest dream actually coming true. Why would God kill that dream?*

Let me ask you a question: what Christian cliché would you offer to answer her question? See, there are no easy answers to something like that. Here was a young man—a young couple—who wanted to minister on staff with Word of Life serving in local churches. They could have potentially reached thousands with the good news of the Gospel. Let's be real here—if I was God and was going to allow a young man to die, I would have looked for someone who was evil and useless. I would not take somebody who planned on giving his life away to reach others.

So by now, you're probably saying, "All right, Mike, are you still saying God is love after hearing that story?" Yes, I am. God is love. One of the things that makes God "God" is love, and no circumstance can change that characteristic.

Let's get to the heart of this truth. What does it mean to say, "God is love"? Is He literally love?

Once again the answer is yes: He is love and He loves us. I will go so far as to say that since He is love, people cannot truly love and be loved if they do not know God.

That's a really bold statement. But if God is love and you don't know God, I don't think you can really understand love. God *is* love.

Consider some aspects of His love.

1. **His love has no beginning, end, or limit.** There are people all over the world who have experienced being loved by someone, and eventually that person declared, "I don't love you anymore." But God never reaches a limit of love because He *is* love. He has no limit.

   Imagine standing on a deserted island, looking at the sea that surrounds you. You can only see to the horizon and it is as if there is no end to the water. God's love is beyond that vast sense we get when we cannot see the limits of the sea. Humanly speaking, this is a way we can get a glimpse of what it means to say that God's love is limitless.

2. **God enjoys His creation.** That may sound strange, but God loves us and He enjoys spending time with us. He is our God but also our friend.

I recently took my wife and my granddaughter to Lake Placid to see

Disney on Ice. We had a great time together. I Twittered about it and said "Hey, having a great time!" because I love being with them. On a much grander scale, God loves being with us. If He got to see Disney on Ice with us, He'd want to Twitter about it, too. God's love is active, and He proved it. He sent His Son to die for us, and He is active in our lives. He demonstrates His love every day.

3. **He loves people, not just populations.** One of the most well-known verses is John 3:16. You often see it in the end zone at football games. It says, "For God so loved the world"—that's the populations—"that whosoever"—that's the individual—"believes in Him should not perish, but have everlasting life." He does not just love your youth group, He loves you individually.

When we talk about God's love, we are reminded that it is sacrificial. He died for you and me. He paid the price for our sin. He gave everything for us.

4. **He will never do anything to harm me.** Maybe you are saying, "Yeah, OK, that's what Christians are supposed to say. He would never do anything to hurt me. But, wait a minute, I just heard the testimony—Josh was only twenty-three when cancer ate away his life. What do you mean God would never do anything to hurt us?"

See, those are the real questions that we are asking. Or maybe those are the real questions that we're afraid to ask. I hope to answer a couple of those questions in this chapter.

5. **God's love is not an emotional impulse.** God's love is more than just a feeling of being loved. His love does not change or vary because of circumstances or failure in our lives because it is based on His character, not our conduct.

   What does the Bible say about this? Let's review John 3:16 again, because it fits so well. "For God so loved the world that He gave His only begotten Son, that whoever believes in Him should not perish, but have everlasting life." He loved us that much.

Take a moment and think about any pain, suffering, agony, or tragedy in your life or the life of someone close to you. Now let's compare them to the bigger picture. I want you to weigh them in light of a couple of things. Are you ready?

First, weigh them in light of eternity. We have to weigh these painful situations in light of Who God is and the fact that He is infinite (without limits). Everything seems so big in our lives because we have limits. Events are magnified in our short life spans. Pain takes lifetimes to fade. Things that happen today seem to change everything within our perspective—in our little picture. Because we have limits it is hard for us to understand, to have the big-picture view that God has.

If you were to talk to Jen, she would say to you, "I don't understand." And as we look at life, if she lives to be seventy-five, eighty, or even one hundred years old, she may never understand. That may seem frustrating to you, but when we look at one hundred years of life compared to eternity, it changes our viewpoint. As believers, we measure things by a different standard.

Now, I'm not trying to give you "church-ese" or persuade you to live life with blinders. This doesn't mean you need to just shrug off all these hard questions. I want to challenge you to see the big picture.

During the time I was putting this material together, I passed the date of what would have been my daughter's thirty-first birthday. Honestly, that was a very lousy day for me. I work hard at keeping the big picture, but I can't deny my feelings either. I believe God loves me, but that doesn't mean I'm not human and that I don't still hurt. And it doesn't mean that you won't, either. You do not have to deny the reality of your pain in order to believe that God is love and has an eternal plan.

Consider with me John 15:13: "Greater love has no one than this, than to lay down one's life for his friends." If a friend went so far as to die for you, would you ever question his love or bring up the time when he did something you didn't understand?

Romans 5:5 says that when God comes into our lives, He literally gives us—pours—His love into our hearts and lives.

Romans 5:8 says, "But God demonstrates His own love toward us, in that while we were still sinners, Christ died for us." We were *still sinners*—we were still disobeying God and living a lifestyle that was horrifying to Him, and He gave His Son to die for us.

Second Corinthians 12:9-10 talks about Paul going through a terribly hard situation. You know what Paul's response was? "His [God's] grace is sufficient for me." Paul believed God was caring for him in the middle of all those hardships. The grace that was sufficient to save him was sufficient to keep him, and it's sufficient to keep you, too, and to help you through such times. I can personally verify that.

Romans 8:35-39 is a powerful passage. Paul begins this passage saying, "Who shall separate us from the love of Christ?" Is it going to be tribulation, distress, persecution or famine, peril, sword? His answer is: "Nothing can separate us from the love of God." Not tragedy, not pain, not leukemia. Nothing! Nothing can separate us from the love of God.

First John 4:8 says, "He who does not love does not know God, for God is love."

I think it's interesting to note that you cannot flip the phrase "God is love" and say "love is God." There is no article; it does not say, "God is the love" or "the God is love." It just says very simply, "God is love." Without the article *the* in any of these places, you can't just flip it to say "love is God" because that's not true. God is more than just love.

First John 4:10 says, "In this is love, not that we loved God, but that He loved us and sent His son to be the propitiation [payment] for our sins." First John 4:19 goes on to say, "We love Him because He first loved us." Revelation 1:5 says, "From Jesus Christ, the faithful witness, the firstborn from the dead, and the ruler over the kings of the earth—to Him who loved us."

The Bible is extremely clear, but we must choose to believe it. We all know people who have a lot of knowledge or know a lot about something, but it's not until they believe the truths that the knowledge changes their life and helps them live the facts they know. We can't do anything to make people believe—they have to make that choice on their own.

But *we* can make the choice to believe these truths ourselves, to let them sink in and give us real answers to our difficult questions.

I have chosen to believe that the Word of God is true, and that it is the foundation for life. The Bible says that God loves and that He willingly died and rose again to give me eternal life. It says that He loves me so much that He cares for me and watches over me every day.

You know what, my friend? Everything in your world may fall apart, but you can be secure knowing that everything you know about God is still true. This will not come because of a feeling; it will come because you come to a place of saying, "I believe this is truth."

So how does this apply to me? In other words, so what? What does it matter to me that God loves me? How does that affect my life?

One way to answer this is to look at Christ's payment for our sin. That salvation act personally applies to and connects with all of us. God offers you the free gift of salvation.

God loves us regardless of our condition. This is great news for us as believers who consistently fail and give into sin. In fact, God loves us in spite of our condition. He doesn't approve of it, but He loves us. The fact that we walk away from Him or make a choice contrary to His Word doesn't change His love for us one bit. That's huge!

God's love is based on His nature, not on our value. None of us could ever do anything to merit the kind of love that God offers. That is fantastic news, to know that His love for me is based on His character, not mine. What a great truth!

God loves us even though His love may not be reciprocated. Reciprocated means *returning love that's been shown to us*. Sometimes we refuse to reciprocate God's love. We are accustomed to dealing with people who will love us back if we love them. But God loves us even when we don't love Him back. Remember Romans 5:8? "God demonstrates His own love toward us, in that while we were still sinners [even when we didn't love Him, even when we didn't care for Him], Christ died for us."

God, Who is love, always allows Himself to love sinful people. That's grace! The reason believers can love each other and those who are without Christ is because they love God, and His love has been poured in their lives. What a comforting truth.

God shows His love for His children in trials. In the good times and the hard times, God is near. You may be in a home where you are being abused, you may face rejection, you may be dealing with the divorce of your parents. To you I can say, God loves you and is near. The reality is that you are hurting, but God does care.

I'm not trying to get you to just dismiss your pain as if it is no big deal, or to quit asking the penetrating questions. Ask those questions, but look for the answer in the only One Who has them: God. Reflect on the truths in this chapter; go over the verses that talk about God's love. Look for ways God shows His love in your everyday life. Don't look for all the pieces to fit easily together just right—look for God's presence instead.

How are you going to process this in your life? This is the "so what?" part. Now what? What are you going to do with this truth? As we have discussed before, there are a couple of things that you can do.

1. You can compartmentalize this.

You can suppress the truth and choose to not believe. You can read these truths about God being love but choose to not let them be part of your life. You can attempt to create your own god, and try to make that god fit into your own small world.

Remember how we talked about trying to fit a big guy into an extra small shirt? It doesn't work! In the same way, you cannot fit an infinite God into your finite mind. He won't fit! The only way that you are going to be able to comprehend this and deal with it is to understand that God is bigger than your pain. God is bigger than your tragedy. God is bigger than your heartache. You're not going to be able to shrink Him to an understandable size; you need to trust Him.

2. You can spiritualize these truths.

This is where you acknowledge the truth, but the clichés are pulled out and applied liberally. You accept them in your head and apply them sporadically to different parts of your life, but it's really just extra information to you—it doesn't run your life.

In order to make true application, we must deal with the truth in our hearts. You cannot make personal application if you just spiritualize.

3. You can internalize the truth.

Don't compartmentalize. Don't spiritualize. Internalize it! Believe the truth. You know what that means? It means that we trust God's character.

Have you ever read *The Lion, the Witch, and the Wardrobe*? I want to remind you of a scene in the book where C.S. Lewis highlights a comforting concept.

The children are about to meet Aslan, and through their conversation with Mr. and Mrs. Beaver, it becomes evident that they are apprehensive about their personal encounter with the King. So, one of them, Lucy, asks, *"Is he a man?"*

"Aslan, a man?" Mr. Beaver says sternly. "Certainly not. I tell you, he is the King of the wood, the son of the great emperor beyond the sea. Don't you know who the King of the beasts is? Aslan is a lion. The great lion."

"Oh," Susan says, "I thought he was a man. Is he quite safe? I shall rather feel nervous about meeting a lion."

"That you will, deary, and no mistakes," Mrs. Beaver says, "if there is anyone who can appear before Aslan without their knees knocking, they are either braver than most or else just silly."

"Then he isn't safe?" Lucy asks.

"Safe?" Mr. Beaver asks. "Don't you hear what Mrs. Beaver tells you? Who said anything about safe? Of course he's not safe. But he's good. He's the King."

My friend, God is not always safe, but He's always good and He always loves us.

Let's revisit the story of Jen and Josh that I introduced at the beginning of the chapter.

> *A year later I can look back and still feel the hurt. I miss Josh. I miss his voice, his touch, his laugh, his special way with people, and his deep insight into the Word of God. Why did God take Josh? I don't know exactly how to answer that question, but I do know that God has taught me what His faithfulness looks like.*
>
> *God was faithful to me after Josh passed away, through the people that surrounded me with love, prayers, and lots of hugs. Above everything else, God used His Word to bring comfort to me. I understand now that Josh is so much better off. He feels no more pain and he will never be sad again. Josh is living in paradise with the God that He loved and served so faithfully.*
>
> *I don't have all the answers to why this happened to me, but I do know that God does, and that He is going to use my life to impact others. Where was God when Josh was dying? Well, for Josh, God was waiting at Heaven's gates to welcome Josh into glory. For me, God was right by my side, loving me, encouraging me, and letting me know that this was His plan for my life, and that He was in total control of everything.*
>
> *God knew what He was doing when He took Josh. Josh was never mine. I'd given Him over to the Lord when we'd first started dating. I may never know why Josh died, but I have faith that God has an amazing plan for my life. I don't know what it is or what it'll look like, but I can't wait to see what He has in store.*

Wow. This isn't a made-up story designed to play at your emotions. It's true. It's a raw yet vivid reminder of the hope we have as believers when we embrace the truth that God is love.

Jen really believes God is love. How about you?

Chapter 6

Wisdom

Mike Calhoun

When crisis intersects with our lives, often the first question is, "So where was God when all of this was happening?" Some believers respond from a foundation of faith, while others lose their spiritual footing as if they were in an earthquake. All of us have or will have tragedies or at least know someone who does. The question is how to respond to problems and pain.

Jeremy Camp wrote his song *I'll Walk by Faith* when his wife died after only four months of marriage. He chose to respond to pain by trusting God. But many other people devastated by crisis question their faith. I don't mean this in a judgmental way—this is a natural response to difficult situations we don't understand.

In any given church, you will have believers on both sides of this extreme. Some have gone through deep waters and have said, "This is tough. I don't know how to exactly deal with it. There is no answer, humanly speaking. I must walk by faith."

Others facing the same type of crisis are just not spiritually capable of exercising their faith. The questions and doubts have replaced any answers they thought they had before the pain came.

My desire is that this chapter will reinforce you if you have chosen to walk by faith. But I also want to gently guide you if you are overwhelmed by the pain, to show you a safe place of rebuilding your trust in God. I would like to meet you at your deepest sorrow and extend a hand to help.

In each of the eight chapters, we've dealt with hard questions that start with "Where was God when ?" We have tried not to give you a quick-fix answer or Christian cliché. I want to continue that mode of operation in this section on the wisdom of God.

I want to lead you to a place where you can make an informed choice about walking by faith or not. We have to come to a place where we decide that, even though our feelings are ragged and our faith is shaky, we want to come back to one Person: the One Who does not change.

Here's the bottom line: I cannot make you believe the Bible is true or that God is all-wise; you have to come to a point where you either say, "I believe that," or "No, I don't." My goal is not to try to convince you to believe anything. My goal is to give you information and introduce a way of thinking that God says will help you believe Him, and that you will see the truth in what He says about Himself.

So let's begin talking about God's wisdom.

God is all-wise, which means He has no need to learn and cannot learn. If He can learn, He is not God. God is never amazed or surprised, and He is never caught off-guard, because He knows all things.

God being all-wise, of course, conflicts with what we see as reality. We have questions. Maybe you have a friend who is dealing with crisis and you're asking, "Why did this happen?" Or, "If God does not need to learn and His ways are always perfect, then why does He seem to be making all of these mistakes?"

You are not the only person living in this place with these questions. You are not alone in your doubts, nor are you alone in your pain.

Others are asking the same types of questions, such as:

- If God does not need to learn and all of His ways are perfect, then why do I feel the need to question if He really does have all the knowledge?
- If God is perfect and His ways are perfect, then why did He allow this tragic situation to happen in my life? I mean, after all, if He really is God and He really is wise, He really knows everything, and He never needs to learn anything, then why did He let this happen to me?
- If God is really wise and His ways are really perfect, then why does the world seem to be so out of control?
- If God's ways are perfect and He cannot learn, then why does He let people do bad things? Is He just stuck in stupid-mode, unaware that people are planning to do evil stuff? Why does He let a father go in and kill all of his children before shooting himself? Why does He let all of this happen?
- If God's ways are perfect and He cannot learn, then why doesn't He fix everything and everybody? Why doesn't He just sprinkle some kind of special magic dust on them and make everyone good?

Here's a testimony I want you to read.

They're calling it the storm of the century, but they said that about Katrina, too. Living in Florida all my life, you'd think I'd know more about hurricanes. All I know is that before the power went out, it was the biggest, meanest-looking storm I'd ever seen on the news.

We can't leave. Poverty and arrogance are a deadly combination in a mandatory evacuation—too poor for the gas and too proud to ask for help. I don't know what's going to happen, but it certainly looks like my chances of dying are pretty high. We live in a mobile home. They were predicting two hundred mile-per-hour winds an hour ago before the power went out. Winds like that could tear our house apart.

Why would God allow something like this to happen? How can He expect me to trust Him when it seems like my world is—literally—falling apart? When God created this world, wouldn't He know that this planet would generate storms like this? Was this storm just an accident or did He just forget about me? I wish I knew what was going to happen when the hurricane comes. Sometimes I don't want to trust God. I just want to know what's going to happen and have this fear of not knowing gone.

Many of us have felt that way. "I just don't know. It doesn't make sense. I don't know what's going to be next. What's going to happen to me? Why in the world would God let this happen? He knew when He created this world that storms like this would happen, right?" We feel this way about huge events that may seem outside our control—such as hurricanes—or even personal events, where it seems like God changing a few details or a few people's decisions could help everything. How could He let this happen if He knew enough to change it? Is He really wise?

Let's look at what it means when we say that God is all-wise. A.W. Tozer says wisdom is "the ability to devise perfect ends and achieve those ends by the most perfect means." In other words, God can see the end from the beginning. He doesn't make mistakes. He can devise the perfect means and then the perfect way to get to those means.

Here is what it means to say that God is all-wise.

His understanding is infinite. In other words, He has no limitations.

God is wise in Himself. In other words, God does not gain wisdom from others. I talk to people I respect and I gain wisdom from them. But God doesn't gain wisdom from any of us. His way cannot be improved upon. God never has to have a planning session about His plan. God's ways cannot be improved upon. God is all-wise and as such He cannot make a mistake.

Now that's a tough concept for me. Maybe it's a tough one for you, too. Your friend takes his life. Your parents get a divorce. You get abused. You were raped. And you say, "Wait a minute—God doesn't make mistakes?" That's a tough one. But that's what it means to say that God has all wisdom.

He is wisdom by essence, not experience. Now, that's just a fancy way of saying that you learn by doing things, sometimes dumb things. I've learned that you don't grab a stove when it's hot because you'll get burned. You learn other things by doing them. It is called learning by experience. But God doesn't need experience to gain wisdom because He does not need to learn.

God's wisdom is perpetual. It never fades or goes away. Have you ever been talking to somebody and realized you can't even remember the person's name? Or have you ever really studied for a test, I mean *really* studied, and when the test begins, you can't remember a thing? But God's wisdom never fades. It never diminishes.

God is able to accurately judge all things. He never has those situations where He thinks, "Oh, I called that one wrong," or "I should have done more research before I decided that situation was like that."

Let's look at some verses that illustrate these principles.

Proverbs 3:19 says, "The LORD by wisdom founded the earth." In wisdom God founded, created, and established everything.

Proverbs 3:12-31 is a long passage, so we'll just look at some parts. The writer says, "Counsel is mine and sound wisdom. I am understanding; I have strength." The author goes on to say in Proverbs 8, "The LORD possessed me at the beginning of His way." Wisdom is talking here and says, "God possessed me [God had wisdom] when He started out, when He was creating the world." When God created the world, He did so in great wisdom because He *had* wisdom and *is* wisdom.

When we talk about a characteristic such as the wisdom of God, it does not mean that He merely practices that characteristic. It means that He *is* wisdom. He is wise. He's not like a person who can make wise decisions one day then totally blow it the next. Who God is defines what wisdom is.

Look at the rest of this passage. Talking in the voice of wisdom, the passage says, "When there were no depths I was brought forth, when there were no fountains abounding with water. Before the mountains were settled, before the hills, I was brought forth; while as yet He had not made the earth or the fields, or the primal dust of the world. When He prepared the heavens, I was there, when He drew a circle on the face of the deep, when He established the clouds above, when He strengthened the fountains of the deep, when He assigned to the sea its limit, so that the waters would not transgress His command, when He marked out the foundations of the earth, then I was beside Him as a master craftsman; and I was daily His delight, rejoicing always before Him, rejoicing in His inhabited world, and my delight was with the sons of men. Now therefore, listen to me, my children, for blessed are those who keep my ways."

In Psalm 24:1, David talks about God creating the earth. Again, He did so in His wisdom.

Psalm 104:24 says, "How manifold are Your works! In wisdom You have made them all."

God's understanding is infinite. Now, the word *infinite* is not a word with which we are very familiar. But as we previously mentioned, to be infinite is to be without limits. God's wisdom is infinite while our wisdom is finite (limited). If I learn and learn and learn and learn until I die, guess what—I'll still only have limited wisdom. But God's wisdom is infinite.

First Timothy 1:17 says, "Now to the King eternal, immortal, invisible, to God who alone is wise." God is the only Being Who can be called totally wise.

Romans 11:33-36 says, "Oh, the depth of the riches both of the wisdom and knowledge of God! How unsearchable are His judgments and His ways past finding out! 'For who has known the mind of the LORD? Or who has become His counselor?' 'Or who has first given to Him and it shall be repaid to him?' For of Him and through Him and to Him are all things, to whom be glory forever. Amen."

We say that God is wisdom and He can't make a mistake. His wisdom never fades; His wisdom is perpetual. He has wisdom by essence and not by experience. We say all that, and now as we read through all these verses about His wisdom, we come to an important question.

How does that apply to me? Or, so what?

These are great verses, and the Scriptures make a strong case for the wisdom of God. But in the middle of a difficult situation, we may struggle with this truth. God is all-wise and He never makes a mistake, and you hear what the Bible says, but you still find yourself saying, "So what?" What does this have to do with *my* situation? Let me introduce you to some of the benefits of believing that God is all-wise.

This truth gives us security. I can trust that God knows what is best since He not only has unlimited knowledge but also perfectly applies that knowledge with perfect wisdom.

I can talk to some of the most intelligent people in the world and seek their advice, but their best wisdom is still limited. We can have incredible security knowing that we can trust God because His wisdom is unlimited.

We think of Socrates, Plato, and philosophers and other men as being really wise, and they were, but even Socrates, speaking of himself in third person, said, "His wisdom could be summed up in the fact that he knew that he knew nothing." If we compiled all the wisdom of the wisest people of our society, they would have to sum it up the same as Socrates: "All my wisdom has shown me I know nothing."

This truth gives us comfort. I can find comfort in knowing that ultimately God's plan is best for me. When you are faced with those hard things, things that completely rock your world, you can find comfort in knowing He cares and knows what is best for us.

I confess from my heart that, humanly speaking, this does not always make sense. There have been times when I've said, "God, You said Your plan is best, but I want You to know something: I'm not sure."

You go, "Whoa, and you're writing the book?" Yeah, because when we're honest, we admit that all of us struggle at some point in our life. Most everyone I know has gone through times where we say, "I don't understand, and it just doesn't seem to fit." But God's wisdom can give us comfort to get to the place of saying, "OK, God, I do not understand, but I trust You. You are wise, and because You are wise, then I can find comfort that Your ways are perfect."

This truth gives direction. A lot of our frustration comes from discovering God's will. He's planned the best goal for us and He's planned the best path for us to reach that goal. Sometimes we just don't like the plan.

Maybe you've prayed something like I have: "God, I want to be a great Christian. I want to be more like Your Son. I want to be more like Jesus." Then when something happens in my life that I don't like, you know what I find myself saying instead? "What in the world are You doing?"

I don't say it out loud. It's an attitude that's deep in my heart, fighting against the hard situation that has come my way. And then as I seek to know God better, as I read my Bible and pray, I've often understood that God is just answering my prayer of me wanting to be more like Christ. He knows the best goal for us and the best path to get us there. Sometimes it takes us through some potholes, sometimes it takes us through some valleys, and sometimes it takes us through the depths of the sea, but He knows best.

Before you write me off as one of those Christians who refuses to face reality, let me tell you that I have struggled with some of the same questions you face. I've had to come to a final point of deciding that I can either walk by faith, or I can become bitter and say, "God, You blew it, and You really don't know what's going on." I had to make a decision just like you need to.

This is where you have to decide. How does this apply to your life? The challenge is: will you accept His will and stop living by your feelings? As long as we keep living by our feelings, we're going to have issues. When your world falls apart, when everything has been rocked, you've got to go by the one thing you can count on.

A friend of mine wrote an article. Let me share some of it with you:

> *"Do you remember singing, "Happy, happy, happy, happy are the people whose God is the Lord"? I do. It messed me up because I thought difficulty in life was a sign of God's absence.*
>
> *That happens to us because we have this fantasy that Christians do not have problems.*

Trusting Christ and following Him is the best decision you'll ever make in your life, and it will be the most intelligent decision you'll ever make in your life, but it won't be the easiest decision. You're going to have some difficulty, pressures, and strain. But the difference between you and the person who walks away from God is that you will never be alone."

My friend who wrote the magazine article also said, "We need to help the students meet the unchanging God Who is in the midst of the suffering rather than invent a god that makes sense at the moment."

We have to quit trying to invent our own god. We'd like to have a god that makes everything seem OK instead of facing reality, but that is only a temporary solution.

This is where we apply this truth to our lives. You have heard that God is all-wise. You understand what the Bible says. You understand that His wisdom gives security, comfort, and direction for your life. You understand it's a challenge to stop living by your feelings. Now, what do you do with this knowledge? There are three things you can do.

1. You can compartmentalize it.

When you compartmentalize, when you suppress the truth that God is all-wise, you try to fit the God you see inside your finite mind. You try to find a quick answer to make you feel better rather than digging for the real truth.

If you continue to do this, though, you're going to be a frustrated person.

We create a god that helps us out of jams. We create a god that we attempt to explain. I was on a plane and was sharing Christ with a college student once. He asked, "How would you explain God?" I just looked at him and said, "Without being offensive, can I just answer that question very quickly?" He said sure, so I did. My answer was: "I don't have to."

I said, "Now, let's get back to the point," and we talked about Jesus. Right before we landed, the student made a decision to ask Jesus into his life. Do you know what he said to me? He said, "In the last six months I've had two people talk to me about knowing Jesus personally. Each time I would ask them how they would explain God, and they got off-track trying to answer me. You're the first one that didn't feel compelled to explain God to me."

Me trying to explain God had nothing to do with the truth I know about God; what's important is that I learn the truth, not try to fit God inside my head. Compartmentalizing, or explaining God, takes the focus off of Who God is and instead puts it on how little we understand.

2. You can spiritualize it.

This seems like the better choice, because at least you acknowledge the truth, but it is just as misdirecting as compartmentalization. All we are doing is giving mental assent to the words, but they never become a part of our belief system. People who consistently practice spiritualization live on borrowed faith. They know the clichés and supposed solutions, but they never get the benefit of seeing the truth lived out in their lives. The danger of living on borrowed faith is that it's not an anchor to your soul.

3. You can internalize it.

By now you have realized that this is the obvious and best choice. Internalization means believing and embracing the truth. And by believing it, you literally trust the character of God. Trust is a tough thing. Trust is a very, very difficult thing.

If I were to tell you to play a game where you would drive south on a narrow road at sixty-five miles per hour, and someone else would be on the same road driving north at sixty-five miles per hour, and that when you pass each other, you are only going to have 14 inches between you and the other driver, some of you would decline. But in reality that is what you do every time you get on a small, two-lane road in many mountain villages.

And yet we get in the car and trust that it will be OK. But when I say to you to trust the God Who created the universe, you reply that you just can't. Taking that big step—where we really trust the Truth—is the hard part.

Check out the end of the testimony we saw at the beginning of this chapter.

> *The hurricane was headed right for us. I don't understand what happened. I was sure it was going to be like what you see on TV, you know? Demolish entire neighborhoods, power outages, no water.*
>
> *We lost power, but it wasn't even the worst hurricane I've ever been through. The storm only grazed us. I'm fine. We're all fine. It's so easy to be thankful and say that I trust God now that I know I'm fine. So why is it so hard to trust Him when I feel like I'm left alone in the dark?*

The choice is always ours. Will we rest on the One Who has all wisdom? Will we trust the One Who cares for us and has our best interest in mine? The decision is yours.

Chapter 7

Omnipresence

Ric Garland

Do you ever feel completely alone? You're in the middle of a crowd, but it doesn't feel like anyone else is there. You have family and friends to hang out with, but no one seems to care about you. Even when you work hard to make the right choices, no one notices.

If God is supposed to be everywhere, why do you feel like this?

He doesn't show up when you have to walk, alone, to your classes every day. You don't see Him when you have to watch your parents fight, and He's not there when you have to find a way—all by yourself—to get past the failed test, the criticism from that friend you disappointed, the harsh words from the coach you displeased.

The Bible says God is everywhere, but you feel pretty alone when you're dealing with hurt. He doesn't seem to be there when you're wrongly accused, made fun of, emotionally abused, physically harmed. He didn't seem to be there afterward, when you kept rethinking the pain, over and over.

Here's a story someone shared with me.

It was a warm summer day, just like any other day, and I was swimming with some friends when I got a phone call. My friend Mikey had been jumped by seven guys. We ran over, and I got to see him before he went to the hospital. He was all bloody, one eye closed, face all black and blue, and I couldn't understand it—why the kids just did it for fun. I couldn't understand why they would beat him up. I heard that a couple of my friends where going up to where he got beat up, so I jumped in the car with them. We pulled up and realized that there were a lot more people there than we thought there would be. As we were getting out of the car, everyone just started coming at us. There were too many, so I got back in the car and tried to drive away, but they blocked off the road. They started throwing rocks at the car, and we ended up having to drive through a playground to get away. After that I was even angrier. I asked God, "Why? We don't deserve this, Mikey doesn't deserve this—why?" So we go back to his house and got his older brother, and he called over some of his friends. They pulled up in another car and opened the trunk. It was full of guns. He said we weren't going to use them; they were just in case things got out of hand. So we went out looking for the guys that beat up Mikey again. At this point, I'm thinking that someone has to pay. There has to be justice in this. We pull up and they're waiting for us. We got out of the car, and not much was said on either side. We just started fighting. Someone pulled out a bat, then someone pulled out a gun. I ran as fast as I could. I didn't know if my friends were OK, I didn't know if anyone was dead, but I just asked God, "Where are You? This is not fair."

We've all been in situations where what's happening just doesn't seem right. It doesn't seem fair that innocent people get hurt. And it can really bother us when we have to deal with all these questions and all the unfairness in our lives, and it just doesn't seem like God is there.

Once again, the Word of God has the answers. The Bible teaches us many things about Who God is, and the one we want to focus on in this chapter is **omnipresence**.

Omnipresence is made up of two words: *omni*, which means "all," and *presence*, which you know means being somewhere. So, saying God is omnipresent means that *all* of God is *everywhere* at the same time.

A. W. Tozer, in his book *The Knowledge of the Holy*, quotes a French writer named Hildebert of Tours. He says, "God is everywhere, close to everything, next to everything, over all things, under all things, outside all things, within all, not enclosed, without but not excluded, above but not raised up, below but not depressed, holy above, presiding holy beneath, sustaining holy within filling." This doesn't mean that God is in everything, which would be pantheism, but rather that He is present everywhere. Pantheism tells us to worship different objects because God is in them. But omnipresence tells us that God as a being is not in everything—He's just everywhere.

Dr. Lewis Perry Chafer says it this way, "If we could conceive even a tiny part of the universe where God is not, then He can't be God." God is one hundred percent everywhere. Years ago, Ivory soap used to say, "It's 99.44% pure." I'm thinking, "What's the other .56%?" The advertisers are saying that to show how pure it is. If you look at pure gold or pure silver, or pure anything, they'll usually say it's ninety-nine percent pure. That's the purest they can get. God is one hundred percent everywhere. If He's only 99.44% present, then He is not God.

God fills every crevice, every crack, every closet. Another way to think of this is that any place can be a holy place. God is not just in church. If you are obedient and in fellowship with God, then God is with you. Any place can be a holy place. Now, that's not an excuse for not going to church—there are other reasons for church. It means this: no matter where you are, you can sense and feel the presence of God.

I've found that most people are not comfortable with an omnipresent God. They want a god they can feel and touch, a god they can understand. We want a god that we can control. We want a little genie in a lamp. Most of us aren't interested in an omnipresent God Who is with us wherever we are, all the time. We would rather have a god that we can manage.

What does the Bible say about omnipresence?

> Amos 9:2-3: "Though they dig into hell, from there My hand shall take them. Though they climb up to heaven, from there I will bring them down; and though they hide themselves on top of Carmel, from there I will search and take them; though they hide from My sight at the bottom of the sea, from there I will command the serpent, and it shall bite them."

God is in complete control of the earth and the people on it. It may look like people who do wrong get away with it, but God knows where they are.

> Psalm 139:7-12: "Where can I go from Your Spirit? Or where can I flee from Your presence? If I ascend into heaven, You are there; if I make my bed in hell, behold, You are there. If I take the wings of the morning, and dwell in the uttermost parts of the sea, even there Your hand shall lead me, and Your right hand shall hold me. If I say, 'Surely the darkness shall fall on me,' even the night shall be light about me; indeed, the darkness shall not hide from You, but the night shines as the day; the darkness and the light are both alike to You."

Just like those who do wrong can't escape from God, those of us who know God can't ditch Him either, even if we want to. No matter what we've done, He's still there.

> Jeremiah 23:23-24: "'Am I a God near at hand,' says the LORD, 'and not a God afar off? Can anyone hide himself in secret places, so I shall not see him?' says the LORD; 'Do I not fill heaven and earth?' says the LORD."

> Proverbs 15:3: "The eyes of the LORD are in every place, keeping watch on the evil and the good."

A lot of human authority figures are far away from where the action happens, and they don't see who is doing right and wrong, or interact with the people under them. But God is always near and can see what's happening.

> Deuteronomy 4:39: "Therefore know this day, and consider it in your heart, that the LORD Himself is God in heaven above and on the earth beneath; there is no other."

> Isaiah 43:2: "When you pass through the waters, I will be with you and
> through the rivers, they shall not overflow you. When you walk through the fire, you shall not be burned, nor shall the flame scorch you."

In this verse, God assures us that not only is He *here,* but He's also actively involved in what's happening. We may ask, "Why didn't God stop it?" This verse tell us that God does know what's going on, so now we have to follow the lesson that we've learned before—that God may have reasons for not intervening.

> Matthew 28:20: "Teaching them to observe all things that I have commanded you; and lo, I am with you always, even to the end of the age."

> Hebrews 13:5: "I will never leave you nor forsake you."

Not only is God everywhere, but He has promised to never leave us. You can't guarantee that to anybody. You're human and you don't know what's going to happen. Something out of your control could break your promise. All of us have had our hearts broken because someone has died in an unexpected way or people have changed their minds in their love or emotions toward us. But God has promised, "I will never leave you. I will never forsake you."

So, we know that the Bible says God is everywhere, but what does that mean? Where can you see that in your everyday life?

You can know you are not alone.

If God is omnipresent, you are not alone. God is by your side. I know that it's quite possible that, even in the middle of a crowd, you can feel alone. No one notices you. You meet other people, you say hello, you smile, but you still feel alone.

Regardless of how you feel, though, you can know God is there, and you need to believe in His omnipresence so that even in the middle of strangers, you know God is right there by your side.

You do not need to be afraid.

Have you ever thought about how much of life is motivated by fear? You may think you're not afraid of anything, but we all fear something. We fear the unknown. That's why some people are afraid of the dark. We fear new situations. We fear some parts of the future.

God's omnipresence, though, means you don't have to be afraid. No matter what you're facing, you can face it with God by your side. In the darkness, in a funeral home, in a jail cell, at your job, in the locker room, in the classroom, in a game, living with new people (like when a parent gets remarried)—God says you don't need to be afraid because He is there with you.

You don't need to feel hopeless.

Can you remember times when you felt completely hopeless? Like there wasn't any way to get out of a bad situation or reverse a decision? You just felt like giving up, like nothing you could do would make the situation better. God's omnipresence means that while you may not be able to do anything, Someone Who can is with you. Whether it's having a seemingly hopeless situation get better, or just being comforted while you wait, God's presence should bring you hope.

I'll never forget, some years ago, a friend of mine whose daughter died in a tragic death. I flew down to where it happened. I was just there to try to help him get all the arrangements done. It was interesting, because I didn't know what to say. I knew all these Scripture verses, but it didn't seem right to share a verse with him at the time. I knew all these neat prayers, but they didn't seem right either. So, for the three or four days I was with him, I said very little. I tried to get him a water when he needed a water, went to McDonald's to get him a hamburger when he needed that. I would stand in the hallway at the hospital for hours. I'll never forget what he said to me afterward: "I just found a new definition of love. It's just being there." You've been there, haven't you? You've hurt so bad that you didn't want a Scripture verse right then. You don't want a lecture; you don't want a cliché. You just want someone to be next to you, maybe someone to hold you. You just want someone to be there. God says you don't have to be hopeless, because He's there.

I remember when state troopers came to a school and told a fifteen-year-old girl that her mom and dad finalized their divorce that morning, and she had twenty-four hours to decide who she was going to live with. How was she supposed to know what to do? Where could she go for help? God says, "You don't have to feel helpless. I'm there."

How about a horrible moral failure? You may say, "Man, you don't know my life. I blew it! I got too involved with my boyfriend or girlfriend and I messed up." You don't have to feel hopeless. You know what the amazing thing is? Even when you were going through that horrible moral failure, God was there.

How about an embarrassing stupid attack? Sometimes you do something and then you ask yourself, "You idiot, what were you thinking? Why did you do that?" Even through an embarrassing stupid attack, do you know what I find? God doesn't abandon me. He doesn't step aside. He doesn't say, "Whoa, that was really dumb. I'm going to back away and let you deal with it." God is there the whole time. He says, "I'm here. I'm present." Even when things look hopeless, they're not. He is present even in the worst disasters that you can think of in life.

God's omnipresence means that He is there in the midst of suffering, pain, sickness, sorrow, anger, grief, bitterness, divorce, betrayal, murder, rape, sexual abuse, cancer, AIDS, abortion, warfare, famine, earthquakes, fire and floods, every natural disaster, accidents, personal loss, and even at the moment of death.

Here's what you're wondering right now. You're going, "If that's true, how can God stand there and see someone being raped and not get involved? How can God see someone's body being wrecked by cancer and not do something? How can God stand there and see someone going through great suffering and pain and not get involved?"

Now, we already know God *is* involved from what we've covered in this book. And we know that just because we don't understand doesn't mean God is wrong. Here's the hard part: God's looking from an infinite mind with eternity in view. We're looking at it from a finite mind with a temporal view. We don't understand His big picture of why He lets that happen. Instead, we have to have faith. You and I have to say, "I don't understand, and it hurts. But by faith I'm going to believe that God is here next to me, and for whatever reason that I don't know, it's going to be for His glory and my good."

In Psalm 23, David says, "Though I walk through the valley of the shadow of death, I will fear no evil; for You are with me."

In the book *The God You're Looking For*, Bill Hybels says the following, "God's presence is with you, but you have to make a choice to believe, and I mean really *believe,* that this is true. This conscious decision is yours alone. As the panic rises, you must ask yourself, 'Am I going to trust in His comforting presence? Will I acknowledge His omnipresent reality? Will I allow Him to strengthen my soul, or will I believe a lie and cry out as many do and say, "You are not near; You don't care for me, do You, God?"'" To think that God is not with you is a *lie,* and you must choose to not only accept the truth, but also let it affect how you deal with tough times.

You need to practice the presence of God.

Practicing the presence of God means living just as if He were always beside you, because He is, you know? He is always right beside you, but often we live unaware of Him. You cannot outrun God to get to any place He is not. He knows your sin and you cannot hide. Right now, if you do not know Jesus Christ as your personal Savior, this very thought ought to ring in your ears, because you *cannot* outrun God. You can't out-maneuver God; you can't manipulate God; you can't put Him in a package.

Knowing this ought to make you turn to Him and say, "God, if that's true, then I'm tired of running and I'm coming to you."

If you're a Christian, you should say the same thing. I find that a lot of Christians have secret sins. You're hiding your sin and you're real good at it. Your youth pastor doesn't know it, your parents don't know it, your best friend doesn't know it, but you've got that secret sin that's hidden from everybody and you're thinking you're getting away with it. If we believe in the omnipresence of God, though, God is there every single time you commit that sin. Every time, He is right there, and He knows every detail of every sin that you commit.

You need to realize God is always there to listen.

First Peter 5:7 says, "Casting all your care upon Him, for He cares for you." That word *cares* means He intensely likes you. He likes who you are. He is intensely concerned for you and He wants to hear about your struggles. God is never busy or preoccupied with other issues. If there were a million crises happening all at the same time, and one hundred wars around the world, God would still listen to your prayers as if you're the only one alive. And He *wants* to hear you.

Now that we understand God's omnipresence and we know how this can affect our lives, how will you deal with it? **There are three ways you can process the truth about omnipresence in your life.**

1. You can compartmentalize it.

This means you suppress the truth. Rather than dealing with what you've just learned, you decide to keep living the same way instead of letting what you've learned affect how you see God or deal with problems. These truths are separate from the rest of your life. You may say, "God was not there when it happened. He couldn't just stand there and watch it happen. I won't believe it."

2. You can spiritualize it.

You acknowledge the truth, but, despite knowing that God is there, you don't let that new truth affect your life. You know it's the truth, and you may even repeat it back to someone when giving them advice, but you don't let it change your habits. You don't work on changing your life to recognize that God is there, and you don't let God's presence help the feelings you have when painful situations arise. But remember, you not responding correctly doesn't mean God's not there.

3. You can internalize and believe the truth.

You know why you may think you've never felt the presence of God? You may not have. He's still there, but you may not be able to sense that because there may be sin in your life. When you and I sin, we cut off fellowship with God. We don't cut off the relationship; we just cut off fellowship. It's just like when you have a disagreement with a person. You may be sitting in the same room as them, but it feels like they're a million miles away.

Think about your relationship with God right now. Is there something that you've been bitter at God about? Is there something you've been demanding an answer from Him for? You may have been saying, "God, I'm not going to trust You until You answer this question." If so, your sin, anger, or bitterness is causing you to not sense the presence of God in your life.

If you want the presence of God, You need to confess your sin of unbelief. All sin comes from unbelief—that's why we sin, because we don't believe God and what He says in His Word. We don't believe that He's there, or that He's good, or that He knows what's happening.

James chapter 4, though, says that when we confess our sin, God comes close to us. God doesn't want to be a God up there in Heaven somewhere, with us hoping we can sense Him. God wants to be a God that's right here, present in you.

Isaiah 41:10 says, "Fear not, for I am with you; be not dismayed, for I am your God. I will strengthen you, yes, I will help you, I will uphold you with My righteous right hand." Look at verse 13: "For I, the LORD your God, will hold your right hand, saying to you, 'Fear not, I will help you.'"

God says He is going to take His right hand and hold our right hand in it. That would look weird—walking down the mall with my wife, with both of us holding each other's right hand. Think about that. You always see someone holding the opposite hand than you! Why would God say that? There's another way to hold my wife's right hand. If I go behind her and wrap my arm around her body and tuck her in real close, then I can hold her right hand with my right hand.

Do you know what is cool about this? My wife's head in on my chest and she can hear my heart beat. When you allow God to draw you in and bring you in close, you can hear the heartbeat of God and follow His will.

As you read this, your heart may be bleeding. You have been through horrible situations in life—probably some things I can't imagine. You're probably feeling so alone. But think about what all these verses are saying: God is there. He wants to bring you in; He wants to bring you close.

Remember the young man's story earlier? He ended by asking, "Where was God?"

> *Looking back on that day, I don't know why Mikey got beat up, and I don't know what happened to the people involved. I do know that it wasn't about God being fair. If life was about being fair, Christ wouldn't have died for all of us, and we'd all be in Hell. But God gave us grace. He gave us free will, and we decided to fight and shoot at each other. But really, more than that, I think it was a chance for me to tell them about what Christ did for them and I failed. Yeah, I was angry, and I didn't understand why it was happening, but I don't deserve Heaven any more than they do. So why should I not give them a chance, too? If I ever get another chance to see them, maybe next time I can tell them about the good news and not fight and shoot them, because that's what this world needs.*

Chapter 8

Omnipresence

Ric Garland

I don't think she ran away. There would be no reason to run away now that finals are over. I may have thought that before she took her Calculus exam, but not now. I don't know where my baby girl is now. Graduation is tomorrow and she disappeared yesterday. She was home alone for less than an hour, and now she's gone.

I don't think she ran away, but I really can't imagine her being taken either. Not her, not in this town. This kind of thing just doesn't happen in this town, especially not to my Anna. She is strong and brave and fearless like her mother.

No clothes missing, car still in the driveway, no signs of struggle. The police say they are doing everything they can. They came here, poked around, went through her stuff, asked a lot of questions, and then classified her as a "missing person."

I only asked them one question: "Where is my little girl?" They couldn't answer me.

Imagining only makes it worse. Some dirty basement? The back of a truck? Way up in the woods somewhere? At the bottom of the lake? She must be terrified—alone, in the dark.

We've been asking "Where was God?" throughout this book, and when we ask that, we're usually thinking, "Why did this happen?" This story has us asking that again—why do situations like this have to happen in a world that a loving, powerful God controls?

The reason we ask is because deep down, we as humans believe in the idea of justice. If we are violated, betrayed, or hurt by anyone in any way, we demand justice. If we are given a punishment we don't deserve, or if we are falsely accused, we expect someone to pay for it.

Our modern court systems do the best they can to make sure there is justice, and the Bible talks about God avenging righteousness and people paying for their actions.

As part of that, we've built up the idea of "rights," sort of as a "no trespassing" sign to protect us from other people hurting or violating us. You know what I'm talking about—there's certain ways you think people should talk to you, or you have opinions on how situations should be handled.

You're probably thinking of some times right now when someone did something to you that you consider an injustice. You may have been dealing with bitterness over this incident recently.

Someone hurt or violated you in a move that was totally unfair, and your heart is overcome with bitterness as you wonder, "Why did this have to happen to me? If God is fair, where was He when this happened? Why is that guy or girl still walking around out there when I feel terrible inside?"

Sometimes it's not something "big" that someone has done to us—it can be as simple as someone ignoring us. Why do they have to shut us out? Your friends start going places without you. Everyone else gets the chance to do something you've always wanted, but you don't get to. Your siblings are treated better than you.

Or maybe you get falsely accused or treated with disrespect for no reason. You worked just as hard, but you don't get the award. You've tried to live a righteous life, but you're stuck dealing with the consequences of someone else's sin. Is that fair? Why do injustices have to happen?

We know the Bible says God is "just" and "merciful." Let's take a closer look at what that means.

The word *justice* or its synonyms appear over eight hundred times in the Bible. The justice of God has to do with the way His character shown—how He deals with people and their actions. Because God is absolutely perfect, His standard of justice is also absolute perfection. While this means we can always count on Him to be totally fair, it also means we are held to His standard. And His standard is a hard one. His justice demands absolute conformity to His perfect character. He cannot have fellowship with unjust people, and His character demands absolute truth.

God's justice demands absolute truth in us—in our conversations, our actions, our thought life, our heart, our motives, our decision-making. God's justice means God gives punishment or reward according to our actions. Think about that. Here's God standard of justice: He says, "Look, if you want Me to be the just Judge, if you want Me to treat people according to how they act, here's My standard: absolute truth in conversation, actions, thought life, heart, motives, obedience." Absolute means *totally*—God can't have any hint of sin.

Here's the reality: if we want a just God and if we want God to be just in all that He does, none of us match up. If we're honest with ourselves, we know that even on a good day, we can't be absolutely right in every way. So when we cry out for justice on this earth, God answers with His justice—a justice that leaves us wanting.

The good news is that God is not only just, but He is also merciful.

Mercy is the *loving-kindness of God.* Another way of putting it is that God does not give us what we deserve. Because of God's perfect standard, we deserve judgment, but God says He is also a loving and kind God.

So, on one hand, every sin must be judged because God is just. Every violation of His standard will be punished. But on the other hand, God is merciful.

Think about the incidents you may be bitter about. You say, "This happened ten years ago, and this person still hasn't been judged!"

Don't worry, it's coming!

Understand this about judgment: the ultimate punishment of sin is Hell. God judges every one of us, and every single one of us has been condemned to Hell because of God's holy justice. God has to do this, because He is a perfect God. He can't choose to send some people to Heaven and some people to Hell, because then some sin would be left unpunished.

The punishment applies to everyone, but that's why God provided salvation for everyone, too—Someone had to pay for that sin.

Without Jesus Christ, we would all have to pay for our sin with an eternity in Hell. But with salvation, we can now choose to accept Jesus' payment for sin and spend eternity in Heaven instead. You don't have to choose the punishment of Hell.

Do you know why people go to Hell? They choose to. God, in a great act of mercy, has provided an alternative—but we have to choose it.

So, while God is completely just—punishing the violations of His absolute standard and not letting anything sinful in His presence—He's also completely merciful—giving us a way to pay for that sin and have an eternity with Him.

Look at what these verses say about God's justice and mercy.

> Psalm 119:137: "Righteous are You, O LORD, and upright are Your judgments."
>
> Psalm 19:9: "The fear of the LORD is clean, enduring forever; the judgments of the LORD are true and righteous altogether."

Psalm 89:14: "Righteousness and justice are the foundation of Your throne; mercy and truth go before Your face."

Isaiah 30:18: "Therefore the LORD will wait, that He may be gracious to you; and therefore He will be exalted, that He may have mercy on you. For the LORD is a God of justice; blessed are all those who wait for Him."

Psalm 103:8-12: "The LORD is merciful and gracious, slow to anger, and abounding in mercy. He will not always strive with us, nor will He keep His anger forever. He has not dealt with us according to our sins, nor punished us according to our iniquities. For as the heavens are high above the earth, So great is His mercy toward those who fear Him; as far as the east is from the west, so far has He removed our transgressions from us.

These verses say that God removes our sins as far as the east is from the west. How far is that? Well, if you're going east, you never go west, and if you go west, you never go east. God's mercy removes all hints of our sin from His just presence, so we can be near Him.

Romans 3:26 (NLT): "For He was looking ahead and including them in what He would do in this present time. God did this to demonstrate His righteousness, for He Himself is fair and just, and He declares sinners to be right in his sight when they believe in Jesus."

Zechariah 7:9: "Thus says the LORD of hosts: 'Execute true justice, show mercy and compassion everyone to his brother.'"

Matthew 23:23: "Woe to you, scribes and Pharisees, hypocrites! For you pay tithe of mint and anise and cummin, and have neglected the weightier matters of the law: justice and mercy and faith. These you ought to have done, without leaving the others undone."

What we're saying is that God is just and faithful. But how does this apply to me? **How does the justice and mercy of God affect our lives?**

God's justice and God's mercy meet in a unique place.

We just talked about how God's mercy brought salvation to everyone through Christ, and that's really the heart of the matter. God's justice and mercy meet at a unique place, at the place of God's judgment—Hell—and it's by studying Hell that we can really learn how justice and mercy work together. For those who choose Heaven, they get to experience God's mercy. But God's justice requires this place called Hell.

I want to take you through a brief journey of Hell because I think sometimes, in so many places, Hell is more of a curse word, even in churches, than something we preach about. Many of you hear Hell as a cliché, but I want you to know that God did create a real place called Hell, because sin must be judged. So let's put aside the cliché images and think of how Hell fits in with a fair, righteous God Who judges sin.

Let me give you a description of Hell.

In Luke 16:24, we find that Hell is a real place with great physical pain.

In Luke 13:28, the Bible says that in Hell, there will be weeping. How did you feel last time you heard somebody weep? Weeping is a sound, an image that grips us. Hell will be a very upsetting place.

Matthew 13:42 says Hell is a place where there's wailing. Think about what wailing sounds like. It's a grotesque sound. It frightens and offends us. We don't hear much of it around here, but in other parts of the world, wailing is common in mourning. It's a guttural sound of people just really weeping right from their souls.

Not only is there weeping and wailing, but Matthew 13:42 says there is a gnashing, or grinding, of teeth. Why? Why do we gnash our teeth? It's because of anger and frustration. It's a defense from crying. You see, people in Hell will be so desperate and they will be in so much pain, that they'll be weeping, wailing, and grinding and gnashing their teeth in pain.

Revelation 21:8 says that Hell is a place of fire and sulfur. Have you ever burned yourself on the stove, maybe just on your finger? It hurts! It's all you can think about; you run around looking for ice for that little burn on your finger, and it can hurt for days. Can you imagine being totally engulfed in flames but not being consumed? Can you imagine the intensity of that pain? I had a friend whose uncle was a truck driver; he told a story about going down the road, following another truck. The other driver apparently fell asleep at the wheel or something and went off the side of the road, his truck rolling three times. My friend's uncle got out of his truck and started running to the other guy. The driver was pinned in the truck, and when my friend's uncle got twenty feet from the truck, the truck just engulfed in flames. The man was pinned in, screaming out for help to his last breath. My friend's uncle said he would never forget that scene.

In Hell, people will be totally engulfed in flames. Imagine the intensity of that fire.

Not only that, but the verse says that Hell is also a place of brimstone and sulfur. Do you remember in chemistry class when you burned sulfur? What happened? It's a putrid smell! It burns your eyes. The verse says that Hell is a place where you're in an intense flame, it smells of sulfur, it burns your eyes, you'll be weeping and wailing, and your teeth are grinding because of the intense pain. That's Hell.

Hell is a place with no light. Jude 1:13 says that Hell is a picture of darkness, a picture of no light.

Think about when you turn off lights in a building, how the exit sign seems so much brighter without the other lights on. When the lights go off, your eyes immediately look for light. There is no light in Hell. Imagine that. Imagine a friend or a relative or a neighbor in Hell, screaming and gnashing his teeth in the intense pain. He tries to look, to see anything, but he cannot. He strains, and smoke fills his eyes. Blackness surrounds him, smothers him, suppresses him. Panicked, he kicks his feet and stretches his arms—but he finds nothing. He's exhausted. But he's still there, suffering. Suspended in darkness, he kicks and screams, yet he cannot find anything.

It gets worse: there is no hope in Hell.

You can cope with anything if you have hope. Prisoners last for years, thinking about the day they'll get out. People go through years of recovery, knowing they can eventually overcome an injury. Individuals who have been emotionally hurt wait for time to heal the wounds. But in Hell there is *no* hope. That friend or loved one you know will be able to remember every time he rejected Jesus Christ. He'll remember all his chances.

You see, in Hell, everybody believes in the Gospel. In Hell, there are more people who believe the Gospel than in your community right now. Here's the problem: it's too late! They scream out and plead for forgiveness. They hope for forgiveness, but it's too late!

Revelation 14:11 says that in Hell there's no rest day or night.

Any situation can be tolerated with rest, a reprieve, a bit of water on your finger. But the reality of eternal torture is that there's not even a tiny bit of reprieve.

Matthew 25:46 says that Hell is eternal. That's forever and ever and ever. You can't get out on probation; you don't get out on good behavior. It's forever and ever and ever.

That is the reality of Hell. Every day people are dying and going to Hell. Every *second* people are dying and going to Hell. Do you know why? Because God is just, and sin *must* be paid for. He's always fair. All the terrible things happening in the world—the children being abused, the genocide, the deceit and lies—that's how it's being paid for. The injustices you face every day? That's how it's being paid for. Hell takes care of making life "fair."

So how does this understanding affect us?

We must understand God's hatred for sin.

Hell is justice for all who sin. Do you hate sin like God does?

How often do you shrug off sin? Do you see someone making fun of someone else, devaluing God's creation, and just let it go? How about little white lies or taking small things that aren't yours? Do you justify lying and stealing, or do you see it as God does—sin that you would avoid if you were as serious about righteousness as He was?

How often do you justify sin, to make yourself feel better about doing what you want, instead of holding it up to God's standard and realizing it *will not* please Him?

We don't have the fear of God in our hearts anymore. We don't see Him as a perfect, righteous God Who hates sin. We act like we can do these wrong things, and He'll just let them slip by; or we forget about what He thinks altogether, and just do those wrong things without a second thought.

Years ago, we used to talk about Christian cussing. Like you shouldn't say "Oh my gosh" because it's slang for "Oh my God." Nowadays, you go into an average youth group, and you hear any kind of curse word. You know why? Because we don't have the fear of God in our hearts anymore.

You find Christians are involved in just about every sin that unsaved people are. Why? Because we don't hate sin like God does. We need to go back to realizing that there is a real place called Hell, because God has a hatred for sin and His hatred for sin goes to the point of sending people to Hell. This is a God Who created these people and loves them, yet their sin is *so* offensive, He sends them to Hell. If we're going to understand God's justice and God's mercy, we have to hate sin like God hates sin. It should be repulsive to us, and we shouldn't even *think* about making excuses or rationalizing it.

We must understand God's love for the sinner.

Salvation is mercy for all who sin. Do you love sinners like God loves sinners? If we all got God's justice, we all ought to spend eternity in Hell. Yet God in His mercy loved us so much that He not only gave us a way out of Hell but also sent His own Son to provide that alternative.

Despite being delivered from the terrible reality of Hell, though, sometimes, as Christians, we still get bitter. We look at sinful people or people who hurt us, and say that they deserve Hell. How dare we judge? How dare we condemn those for whom God's Son died?

How are we going to process all this? What are we going to do now? What does this mean to us?

There are three things you can do about God's justice and God's mercy—three ways you can handle it in your life.

1. You can compartmentalize it.

Consider these two statements:

- It's easier for me to believe God is angry with me than it is for me to believe He forgives me.

Maybe you're reading this, and you go, "Man, I know what a rotten sinner I am, and I feel God's anger on me. I ought to be judged. It's easier for me to believe God is angry with me than to believe that He can forgive me, even as a Christian."

- I'm grateful for God's mercy, but there are some people I know I could never forgive.

You are grateful for God's mercy, but there are some people in your life that you are just not going to forgive. "That man violated me, and I'm not going to forgive him." "My parents got a divorce, and they don't deserve my forgiveness." "That person did something to me, and I have my rights and I am not going to forgive them. God's mercy or not, I'm not going to do it."

Do you agree with either of these two statements? If you do, you may be ignoring the truth we just talked about—separating what God says from the reality you see in your life. But that doesn't change the truth. If you agree with either of these statements, go back and re-read God's promises about justice and mercy.

2. You can spiritualize it.

That means acknowledging the truth but not really doing anything about it. This is a step beyond not accepting God's justice or mercy; you know it's there, but you don't let it affect you. You say, "I know God is just and merciful, but it doesn't fix my hurt now. I've learned that in Sunday school. God is just, God is merciful, yada, yada. But how does it change the hurt? How does it make me deal with knowing that a person is still living with that injustice out there?"

3. You can internalize God's truth.

We can start believing the truth. Let me take it in two ways. You may be reading this and sweating inside because you know what you've done. You may be filled with guilt, knowing that you are the one who stepped over the boundaries and did the violating. As a Christian, how could God forgive you? There's good news! I want you to know that if you've sinned and felt the conviction of God, this is what you need to do.

1. You need to confess your sin.

Do you know what that means? Agree with God. Confession doesn't mean telling God you know you did it and you got caught. It's not just a way to get guilt off your chest. Here's what it means: you agree with God how putrid, how unholy, and unjust it was, and you agree that you don't deserve God's mercy. Cry out to God. Say, "God, I agree with You that my sin is wicked."

2. Accept God's forgiveness.

You are your own worst enemy; you're saying, "I can't do it. I can't accept God's forgiveness." What you are really saying is that the blood of Jesus Christ was not enough. You're saying Jesus dying on the cross wasn't enough and you need to do more. Forget about yourself and look at the truth: Christ's death is enough. Are you willing to confess your sins to God today? When you confess your sins to Him, He forgives you.

That blows our mind away. You're thinking, "It can't be that easy; it can't be that simple," but it is. God is ready and willing to forgive. All you have to do is say, "God, I agree with You. I know I've sinned," and God will forgive you.

There may be another problem, though; you may be reading this and feel condemnation. There is a difference between Satan's condemnation and God's conviction. If you have sinned and you asked God to forgive you, but you still feel condemnation, that's not from God. Romans 8:1 says there is no condemnation to those who are in Christ Jesus. The condemnation you are feeling comes from Satan, because Satan wants to accuse you and put you down because he hates you. If he had his way, he would destroy you. The Holy Spirit of God convicts, and that conviction is to bring you to freedom. Condemnation is not from God; it's from Satan.

Now, you may not be dealing with conviction about your own sin; you may be in the other group—someone who is still hurting from when someone sinned against you. In that case, you need to apply God's mercy and justice by forgiving others.

As you've been reading this, you may be thinking, "It's great that God has given everyone mercy and forgiven them, but I've still been hurt. My rights have been violated. There's been injustice and it was *not fair* what happened."

Think about what the Bible says in 1 Corinthians 6:19-20. It says your body is the temple of the Holy Ghost. God bought you and all of your rights are His. That human "right" you have to be angry about injustice? That's not yours anymore—you are now serving a totally just God. You need to give your rights back to God. He saved you and promises to protect you; He promises to punish sin. You need to let Him do that. Forgiveness is to release the debt someone owes you and give it to God and let Him do what He pleases.

You have to give it completely to God: "Dear God, this man violated me. You know what he did, but I'm going to forgive him. I'm releasing the debt to You. If You want to kill him, kill him. If You want to bless him, bless him. If You want him to get saved, let him get saved. God, You do what You will. It's out of my hands. I'm too emotional and too sinful to figure it out, so I'm going to release the debt he owes, and I'm going to give it to You, and I'm going to let You handle it."

This may not be a one-time thing. You may need to do it a thousand times. Every time the pain comes up, every time the memory comes up, you have to say again, "God, You're God, and I'm giving this to You to handle." He's God—He'll know what's best for that situation. Realize that as long as you're bitter toward that person, you are a slave to that person. They still control you. Your ability to love and serve God, and love and serve others, is held in bondage when you can't forgive someone who hurt you.

Remember our story at the beginning of this chapter? Let's continue.

It's been two years since Anna disappeared. She would have been twenty-one today. I still have these dreams about her. I wonder what she would have done with her life. She could have been a missionary, or a pastor's wife; she could just as well have been a dental hygienist or a teacher. You never could tell what was going to strike her fancy.

The sky is gorgeous tonight. You know, on nights like this I can't help but wonder, "Maybe Anna's seeing what I can see." You know, I don't understand, but it really does help to know that wherever she is, whether she is in Heaven or on the other side of the earth, God is right there with her. She can pray and talk to Him whenever she wants. He has never left her side, just like He has never left mine.

Our human nature wants to continue to ask the "why" questions. God wants to show us Who. For all that others have hurt us, He wants us to experience His mercy and a relationship with Him—Someone Who will never hurt us. He's willing to forgive us. Are you willing to forgive yourself? Are you willing to forgive others?